South Africa, Lesotho & Swaziland

a Lonely Planet travel atlas

South Africa, Lesotho & Swaziland – travel atlas

1st edition

Published by

Lonely Planet Publications
Head Office: PO Box 617, Hawthorn, Vic 3122, Australia
Branches: 155 Filbert St, Suite 251, Oakland, CA 94607, USA
10 Barley Mow Passage, Chiswick, London W4 4PH, UK
71 bis rue du Cardinal Lemoine, 75005 Paris, France

Cartography

Steinhart Katzir Publishers Ltd
Fax: 972-3-699-7562
email: 100264.721@compuserve.com

Printed by

Colorcraft Ltd, Hong Kong
Printed in China

Photographs

Glenn Beanland, Richard Everist, Di Jones (Malealea Lodge), Jon Murray, Micky Reilly (Big Game Parks of Swaziland), Luba Vangelova

Front Cover: Beach huts at Muizenberg, Cape Town (Jon Murray)
Back Cover: Telephone wire basket, Soweto (Glenn Beanland)
Title Page: Niche at art gallery painted in Nobele style (Jon Murray)
Contents Page: King Protea (Luba Vangelova)

First Published

May 1997

National Library of Australia Cataloguing in Publication Data

Murray, Jon
South Africa, Lesotho & Swaziland travel atlas.

1st ed.
Includes index.
ISBN 0 86442 443 4.

1. South Africa - Maps, Tourist. 2. South Africa - Road maps.
3. Lesotho - Maps, Tourist. 4. Lesotho - Road maps.
5. Swaziland - Maps, Tourist. 6. Swaziland - Road maps.
I. Murray, Jon. (Series : Lonely Planet travel atlas).

912.68

Contents

Jon Murray

Jon Murray spent some years alternating between travelling and working with various publishing companies in Melbourne (Australia). He joined Lonely Planet as an editor but was soon travelling again, this time researching guidebooks. He is co-author of Lonely Planet's *South Africa, Lesotho & Swaziland* and author of *New South Wales & the ACT*. He has updated several other Lonely Planet guides, including *Papua New Guinea* and sections of *Australia*. He lives in Melbourne but spends a lot of time battling blackberries on his bush block near Daylesford.

About this Atlas

This book is another addition to the Lonely Planet travel atlas series. Designed to tie in with the equivalent Lonely Planet guidebook, we hope the *South Africa, Lesotho & Swaziland travel atlas* helps travellers enjoy their trip even more. As well as detailed, accurate maps, this atlas also contains a multi-lingual map legend, useful travel information in five languages and a comprehensive index to ensure easy location-finding.

The maps were checked on the road by Jon Murray as part of his preparation for a new edition of Lonely Planet's *South Africa, Lesotho & Swaziland* guide.

From the Publishers

Thanks to Danny Schapiro, chief cartographer at Steinhart Katzir Publishers, who researched and drew the maps with the assistance of Michal Pait-Benny and Iris Sardes; Iris also prepared the index. At Lonely Planet, the maps and index were checked and edited by Lou Byrnes, with assistance from Paul Smitz. Louise Klep was responsible for all cartographic checking, design, layout, and cover design. The back cover map was drawn by Paul Clifton. Illustrations by Matt King.

Lou Byrnes coordinated the translations. Thanks to translators Yoshiharu Abe, Christa Bouga-Hochstöger, Adrienne Costanzo, Pedro Diaz, Megan Fraser, Elisabeth Kern and Nick Tapp.

Request

This atlas is designed to be clear, comprehensive and reliable. We hope you'll find it a worthy addition to your Lonely Planet travel library. Even if you don't, please let us know! We'd appreciate any suggestions you may have to make this product even better. Please complete and send us the feedback page at the back of this atlas to let us know exactly what you think.

From left to right: Reedbuck, Klipspringer, Hartebeest and Lesser Kudu

South Africa,
Lesotho & Swaziland
0
50
100 km
Namibia
Botswana
Mozambique
Swaziland
Lesotho
Atlantic
Ocean
Indian
Ocean
Northern Province
North-West
Gauteng
Mpumalanga
Free State
KwaZulu/
Natal
Northern Cape
Eastern Cape
Western Cape
Messina
Louis Trichardt
Thohoyandou
Giyani
Ellisras
Pietersburg
Tzaneen
Phalaborwa
Potgietersrus
Thabazimbi
Nylstroom
Temba
Lydenburg
Sabie
Hazyview
Zeerust
Rustenburg
Mmabatho
Mafikeng
PRETORIA
Nelspruit
Komatipoort
Middelburg
Barberton
Lichtenburg
Witbank
Pigg's Peak
JOHANNESBURG
Bethal
Ermelo
Mbabane
Manzini
Potchefstroom
Vryburg
Vereeniging
Standerton
Klerksdorp
Hlathikulu
Ndumu
Kuruman
Vrede
Lavumisa
Bloemhof
Vaal River
Kroonstad
Louwsburg
Welkom
Christiana
Newcastle
Vryheid
Mkuze
Upington
Bohlakong
Harrismith
Dundee
Bethlehem
Ulundi
St. Lucia
Fiksburg
Ladysmith
Mtubatuba
KIMBERLEY
Empangeni
Estcourt
BLOEMFONTEIN
Ladybrand
Richards
Bay
MASERU
Port Nolloth
Pofadder
Nababeep
Springbok
PIETERMARITZBURG
Stanger
Prirska
Mafeteng
DURBAN
Quthing
Qacha's Nek
De Aar
Colesberg
Aliwal North
Kokstad
Port Shepstone
Calvinia
Noupoort
Barkley East
Middelburg
Umtata
Elliot
Clanwilliam
Queenstown
Port St. Johns
Graaff Reinet
Cradock
Sada
Beaufort West
Vredenburg
Citrusdal
Somerset East
Fort Beaufort
Bisho
Saldanha
King William's Town
EAST LONDON
Grahamstown
Worcester
Oudtshoorn
Montagu
Knysna
Uitenhage
Port Alfred
Stellenbosch
George
CAPE TOWN
Swellendam
Plettenberg Bay
Jeffreys Bay
PORT ELIZABETH
Mossel Bay
Hermanus
10
11
12
14
15
16
17
18
19
20
21
22
23
24
25
26
27
28
29
30
31
32
33
34
35
36
37

16°E
17°E
18°E
19°E
20°E
21°E
22°E
23°E
23°S
Tropic of Capricorn
24°S
25°S
26°S
27°S
28°S
29°S
30°S
31°S
32°S
33°S
34°S
Botswana
Namibia
Kalahari Gemsbok National Park
Richtersveld National Park
Augrabies Falls National Park
Orange River
Atlantic Ocean
Olifants River
Cederberg Wilderness Area
Karoo National Park
Touws River
Cape of Good Hope Nature Reserve
De Hoop Nature Reserve
Wilderness National Park
Upington
Pofadder
Port Nolloth
Nababeep
Springbok
Prirska
Calvinia
Clanwilliam
Citrusdal
Vredenburg
Saldanha
Beaufort West
Ceres
Touws River
Malmesbury
Worcester
Montagu
Robertson
Oudtshoorn
CAPE TOWN
Stellenbosch
Swellendam
Riversdale
George
Knysna
Somerset West
Caledon
Mossel Bay
Plettenberg Bay
Hermanus
Bredasdorp
R375
R379
R380
R31
R360
N14
R359
N8
R358
N7
R382
R355
R383
R27
R361
R357
R386
R353
R63
R363
R354
R356
R381
R366
R303
R44
R45
R46
R318
R43
R60
R62
R323
R327
R328
R324
R322
R317
R316
R332
N1
N12
R407
R341
N2
N10
R384
R403
R398
R385
R369
R387
R61
N9
Major Highway
Highway
Regional Road
Railway

Zimbabwe
Mozambique
25°E
26°E
27°E
28°E
29°E
31°E
32°E
Messina
Nwanedi National Park
Thohoyandou
Louis Trichardt
Kruger National Park
Giyani
Ellisras
Pietersburg
Tzaneen
Phalaborwa
Potgietersrus
Thabazimbi
GABORONE
Nylstroom
Blyde River Canyon Nature Reserve
Pilansberg National Park
Warmbad
Lydenburg
Hazyview
Sabie
Temba
Zeerust
Rustenburg
Brits
PRETORIA
Nelspruit
Komatipoort
Mmabatho
Mafikeng
Middelburg
Belfast
Witbank
Waterval-Boven
Barberton
JOHANNESBURG
BENONI
Lichtehburg
Carolina
Pigg's Peak
MAPUTO
Carletonville
Breyten
Mbabane
Heidelberg
Potchefstroom
Ermelo
Manzini
Stilfontein
Vanderbijlpark
Vereeniging
Bethal
Klerksdorp
Orkney
Schweizer Reneke
Swaziland
Hlathikulu
Big Bend
Ndumu Game Reserve
Wolmaransstad
Viljoenskroon
Heilbron
Frankfort
Standerton
Piet Retief
Ndumo
Tembe Elephant Reserve
Vaal River
Bothaville
Bloemhof
Vrede
Charlestown
Volksrust
Lavumisa
Kroonstad
Itala Game Reserve
Christiana
Odendaalsrus
Utrecht
Louwsburg
Reitz
Newcastle
Madadeni
Mkuze
The Greater St. Lucia Wetlands
Welkom
Hennenman
Vryheid
Virginia
Bethlehem
Bohlakong
Harrismith
Glencoe
Dundee
Barkly West
Theunissen
Senekal
Umfolozi Game Reserve
The Hluhluwe Park
Moloza River
Brandfort
Winburg
Royal Natal National Park
Golden Gate Highlands National Park
Ulundi
KIMBERLEY
St Lucia
Ladysmith
Mtubatuba
Clocolan
Ficksburg
BLOEMFONTEIN
Tugela River
Empangeni
Richards Bay
Ladybrand
Estcourt
MASERU
Mooirivier
Greytown
Giant's Castle Game Reserve
Lesotho
Howick
Stanger
PIETERMARITZBURG
Tongaat
Verulam
Mafeteng
DURBAN
Mohales Hoek
Qacha's Nek
Mkomazi River
Quthing
Umzinto
Colesberg
Aliwal North
Kokstad
Barkley East
Burgersdorp
Port Shepstone
Noupoort
Indian Ocean
Molteno
Elliot
Middelburg
Mkambati Nature Reserve
Umtata
Queenstown
Port St Johns
Cradock
Coffee Bay
Graaff Reinet
Sada
Mountain Zebra National Park
Great Fish River
Great Kei River
Bedford
Adelaide
Stutterheim
Somerset East
Fort Beaufort
Bisho
King William's Town
EAST LONDON
Kirkwood
Addo Elephant National Park
Grahamstown
Uitenhage
Port Alfred
PORT ELIZABETH
Jeffreys Bay
South Africa,
Lesotho & Swaziland
0
25
50 km

MAP LEGEND

Number of Inhabitants:

JOHANNESBURG	500,000 - 1,000,000
PORT ELIZABETH	250,000 - 500,000
BLOEMFONTEIN	100,000 - 250,000
Uitenhage	50,000 - 100,000
Edendale	25,000 - 50,000
Empangeni	10,000 - 25,000
Potsdam	<10,000
Macleantown	Village

PRETORIA

Capital City
Capitale
Hauptstadt
Capital
首都

Capital City (Locator map)
Capitale (Carte de situation)
Hauptstadt (Orientierungskarte)
Capital (Mapa Localizador)
首都（地図上の位置）

KIMBERLEY

Provincial Capital
Capitale de Province
Landeshauptstadt
Capital de Provincia
地方の中心地

International Boundary
Limites Internationales
Staatsgrenze
Frontera Internacional
国境

Provincial Boundary
Limites de la Province
Landesgrenze
Frontera de Provincia
地方の境界

Major Highway
Route Nationale
Femstraße
Carretera Principal
主要な国道

Highway
Route Principale
Landstraße
Carretera
国道

Regional Road
Route Régionale
Regionale Fernstraße
Carretera Regional
地方道

Secondary Road
Route Secondaire
Nebenstraße
Carretera Secundaria
二級道路

Unsealed Road
Route non bitumée/piste
Unbefestigte Straße
Carretera sin Asfaltar
未舗装の道

Railway
Voie de chemin de fer
Eisenbahn
Ferrocarril
鉄道

Kanus

Railway station
Gare Ferroviaire
Bahnhof
Estación de Ferrocarril
駅

N11 R357

Route Number
Numérotation Routière
Routenummer
Ruta Número
道路の番号

99

Distance in Kilometres
Distance en Kilomètres
Entfernung in Kilometern
Distancia en Kilómetros
距離（km）

International Airport
Aéroport International
Internationaler Flughafen
Aeropuerto Internacional
国際空港

Regional Airport
Aéroport régionale
Regionalflughafen
Aeropuerto regional
地方の飛行場

Airfield
Aérodrome
Flugplarz
Pista de Aterrizaje
飛行機発着場

Seaport
Port de Mer
Seehafen
Puerto Marítimo
港

Cathedral
Cathédrale
Kathedrale
Catedral
大聖堂

Church
Église
Kirche
Iglesia
教会

Mosque
Mosquée
Moschee
Mezquita
モスク

Temple
Temple
Tempel
Templo
寺院

Battle Site
Champ de Bataille
Schlachtstelle
Campo de Batalla
戦場

Fort/Citadel
Château Fort/Citadelle
Festung/Zitadelle
Fuerte/Ciudadela
城・砦

Monument
Monument
Denkmal
Monumento
記念碑

Viewpoint
Point de Vue
Aussicht
Mirador
展望地点

Rest Camp
Cantonnement de repos
Rastlager
Campamento de reposo
休憩所

Camping Ground
Terrain de Camping
Zeltplatz
Camping
キャンプ場

Cave
Grotte
Höhle
Cueva
洞窟

Mafadi 3450 +
Mountain
Montagne
Berg
Montaña
山

Pass
Col
Paß
Desfiladero
峠

Tunnel
Tunnel
Tunnel
Túnel
トンネル

National Park
Parc National
Nationalpark
Parque Nacional
国立公園

Ruins
Ruines
Ruinen
Ruinas
遺跡

Lighthouse
Phare
Leuchtturm
Faro
灯台

River
Fleuve/Rivière
Fluß
Río
川

Lake
Lac
See
Lago
湖

Spring/Well
Source/Puits
Quelle/Brunnen
Manantial/Pozo
泉／井戸

Waterfall
Cascades
Wasserfall
Cascada
滝

Swamp
Marais
Sumpf
Pantano
沼地

Desert
Désert
Wüste
Desierto
砂漠

Salt Lake
Lac Salé
Salzsee
Lago de Sal
塩湖

Tropics
Tropiques
Tropen
Los Trópicos
回帰線

3600 m
3300 m
3000m
2700 m
2400 m
2100 m
1800 m
1500 m
1200 m
900 m
600 m
300 m
0

0 30 60 km

Projection: Universal Transverse Mercator

1 : 1 400 000

A
B
C
D
26°E
27°E
1
2
3
4
5
6
Mmashoro
Mabeleapudi
Serule
Mmadinare
Selebi-Ph
Tamasane
Mogapinyana
Tlhabala
Mogorosi
Serowe
Palapye
Botswana
Malaka
Maunatlala
Mosolotsane
Mokgware Hills
Lerala
Shoshong Hills
Kalamare
Seleka
23°S
Lose
Bonwapitse
Mokobeng
Shoshong
Mahalapye
Machaneng
Lephephe
Sojwe
Makwate
Tropic of Capricorn
Dinokwe
Kudumatse
Limpopo River
Stockpoort
Monte Christo
R510
Oranjefontein
BOTSWANA
SOUTH AFRICA
Mmamabula
Dovedale
Mongol River
Ons Hoop
Maphashalala
Dibete
Ellisras
Masama
Matlabas River
Afguns
Artesia
24°S
Elmeston
Dikolaklolana River
Ngotwane River
Mokolo
Spanwerk
Sekhukhwane River
Mmamanstwe Hill
Rooibokkraal
Rooibosbult
R510
Hermanu
Lentswelatau
Voortrekkerspos
Rasesa
Matlabas
Sentrum
Mochudi
Metsemotlhaba River
Waterberg
2085
Maricosdraai
Silent Valley
Crocodile River
Odi
Mogoditshane
Rankin's Pass
Sikwane
Oostermoed
GABORONE
Tlokweng
Derdepoort
16
17
Thabazimbi
Kopfontein Border Gate
Kayaseput
Dwaalboom
Witfonteinrand Mountain
Bier River
Ben Alberts Nature Reserve
Mabula Game Reserve
Mogonye
Ramotswa Station
Ramotswa
Swartkopfontein Border Gate
Marico River
1499
R511
Rooiberg

E
F
G
H
28°E
29°E
30°E
1
2
3
4
5
6
Zimbabwe
Gubajango
Semolale
Motwon River
Machachuta
Thuli
Tuli Safari Area
Shashi River
Mazunga River
Mtetengwe River
Pazhi River
Bobonong
Motloutse River
Molalatau
Thune River
Sefophe
North-East Tuli Game Reserve
ZIMBABWE
SOUTH AFRICA
Beitbridge
Pont Drift Border Gate
R572
Mathathane
Tuli Block Farms
Platjan Border Gate
R521
Evangelina
Messina
Messina Nature Reserve
Testsebjwe
Baines Drift
Zanzibar Border Gate
Bridgewater
BOTSWANA
SOUTH AFRICA
Kopersspruit
Usutu
Saamboubrug Border Gate
Brombeek
Bandur
Mopane
Sand River
Gregory
Alldays
Huntleigh
Maasstroom
De Gracht
Tonash
Swartwater
Machemma Ruins
Nzhelele Dam
Brak River
Masekwaspoort
Dzata Ruins
Carlow
Oorwinning
Wyllie's Poort
R523
Waterpoort
Grobler's Bridge Gate
Magalakwin River
Southpansberg
Wyllie's Poort Verwoerd Tunnel
Tolwe
Tom Burke
Lesheba Wilderness
1718
Blouberg
Vivo
Buysdorp
R522
Mara
Louis Trichardt
Fort Hendrina
Marnitz
R524
Blinkwater
Sending
Ben-Lavin Nature Reserve
Elim Hospital
Glen Alpine Dam
R578
Baltimore
Woudkop
Northern Province
Bochum
Blouhaak
Sand River
12
Steilwater
Steilloopbrug
Dendron
Legkraal
Bandelierkop
N11
Villa Nora
Janseput
Marken
Botlokwa
Groot Spelonke
Soekmekaar
R36
Kalkbank
Bylsteel
Thorndale
Overyssel
Gilead
R521
Moletzie Bird Sanctuary
Munnik
Mooketsi
Mogalakwenastroom
Matlala
Rita
R81
Duivelskloof
Sebayeng
Limburg
N1
Solmondale
Olyfberg
Politsi
Groesbeek
Seshego
Leshwane
Tzaneen Dam
Mankweng
Tzaneen
Lapalala Wilderness
Mokamole
Mapela
Pietersburg
Magoebaskloof
Melkrivier
R518
R71
Mashashane
Boyne
Haenertsburg
Ebenezer Dam
Sterkwater
Rietkolk
R33
2128
Percy Fyfe Nature Reserve
Sterk River
Mahwelereng
Nuwe Smitsdorp
Gladdeklipkop
Strydpoortberge
Potgietersrus
Makapan's Cave
R37
The Downs
Chuniespoort
Moorddrif Monument
Palala
Vier-en-Twintig Riviere
Drummondlea
R518
R579
Chuniespoort
Zeekoegat
Sterkrivier Dam
Zebediela
R518
Lebowakgomo
Hanglipberg
Haakdoring
R37
Vanalphensvlei
Mineral Springs
N1
R520
Gomples
R579
Naboomspruit
N11
Immerpan
17
18
Nylsvley Nature Reserve
R519
Nylstroom
R101
Middelfontein
Crecy
Roedtan
R516

A
B
C
D
1
2
3
4
5
6
Zimbabwe
Mozambique
ZIMBABWE
SOUTH AFRICA
ZIMBABWE
MOZAMBIQUE
SOUTH AFRICA
MOZAMBIQUE
Beitbridge
Nuli
Diti
Tshiturapadsi
Chipise
Mabalabuta
Malapati
Messina
Messina Nature Reserve
Limpopo River
Pafuri Border Gate
Pafuri Gate
Masisi
Crooks Corner
Pafuri
Luvuhu River
Nyalaland
Tshipise
Honnet Nature Reserve
Minerale Bronne Springs
Nwanedi National Park
Nwanedi Dam
Matavhelo
Nzhelele Dam
Punda Maria
Dzata Ruins
Lake Fundudzi
Sirheni Bushveld Camp
Sibasa
Thohoyandou
Babalala
Mapai
Batombo
Tshakhuma
Mavamba
Borchers
Elim Hospital
Klein Letaba
Kruger National Park
Shingwedzi Camp
Nsami Dam
Klein Letaba River
Ha-Magoro
Giyani
Mamaila
Bateleur Bushveld Camp
Hildreth Ridge
Tropic of Capricorn
Nkomo
Mopani Camp
Mooiplaas
Boulders Camp
Mooketsi
Ga-Modjadji
Duivelskloof
Hans Merensky Nature Reserve
Shimuwini Bushveld Camp
Politsi
Nkambak
La Cotte
Mineral Springs
Groot Letaba River
Tzaneen Dam
Tzaneen
Magoebaskloof
Mulati
Lulekani
Letsitele
Murchison
Namakgale
Phalaborwa
Letaba Camp
Massingir Dam
Massingir
Gravelotte
Leydsdorp
Mohlatsi River
Olifants River
Olifants Camp
Ofcolaco
Balule Camp
The Downs
Mica
Trichardtsdal
Drakensberg
Tshukudu Game Lodge
Umbabat Game Reserve
Roodewal Camp
Klaserie Private Nature Reserve
Manang a Game Reserve
Timbavati
Timbavati Private Nature Reserve
Mazimechopes River
Penge
Hoedspruit
J.G. Strijdom Tunnel
Kapama Game Reserve
Abel Erasmus Pass
Nyala Camp
Satara Camp
Thornybush Game Reserve
Blyde River Gorge Natural Reserve
Echo Caves
Kampersrus
Orpen Gate
Orpen Camp
Sweni River
Nwanetsi Camp
Klaserie
Acornhoek
Talamati
Bubi River
Mwenezi River
Nwanedi River
Njelele River
Sand River
Mutale River
Pafuri River
Mphongolo River
Phugware River
Shingwedzi River
Nsama River
Klaserie River
Timbavati River
Nwanetzi River
Mphongolo River
R525
R508
R523
R524
R81
R578
R36
R529
R71
R526
R40
R37
R527
R531
R532
▼18▼
▼19▼

RICHARD EVERIST

JON MURRAY

JON MURRAY

Top: Nature's Valley near Bloukran's Pass, Eastern Cape Province
Middle: The Camelyard – Helen Martins' Owl House, New Bethesda, Eastern Cape Province
Bottom: Cape Town by night

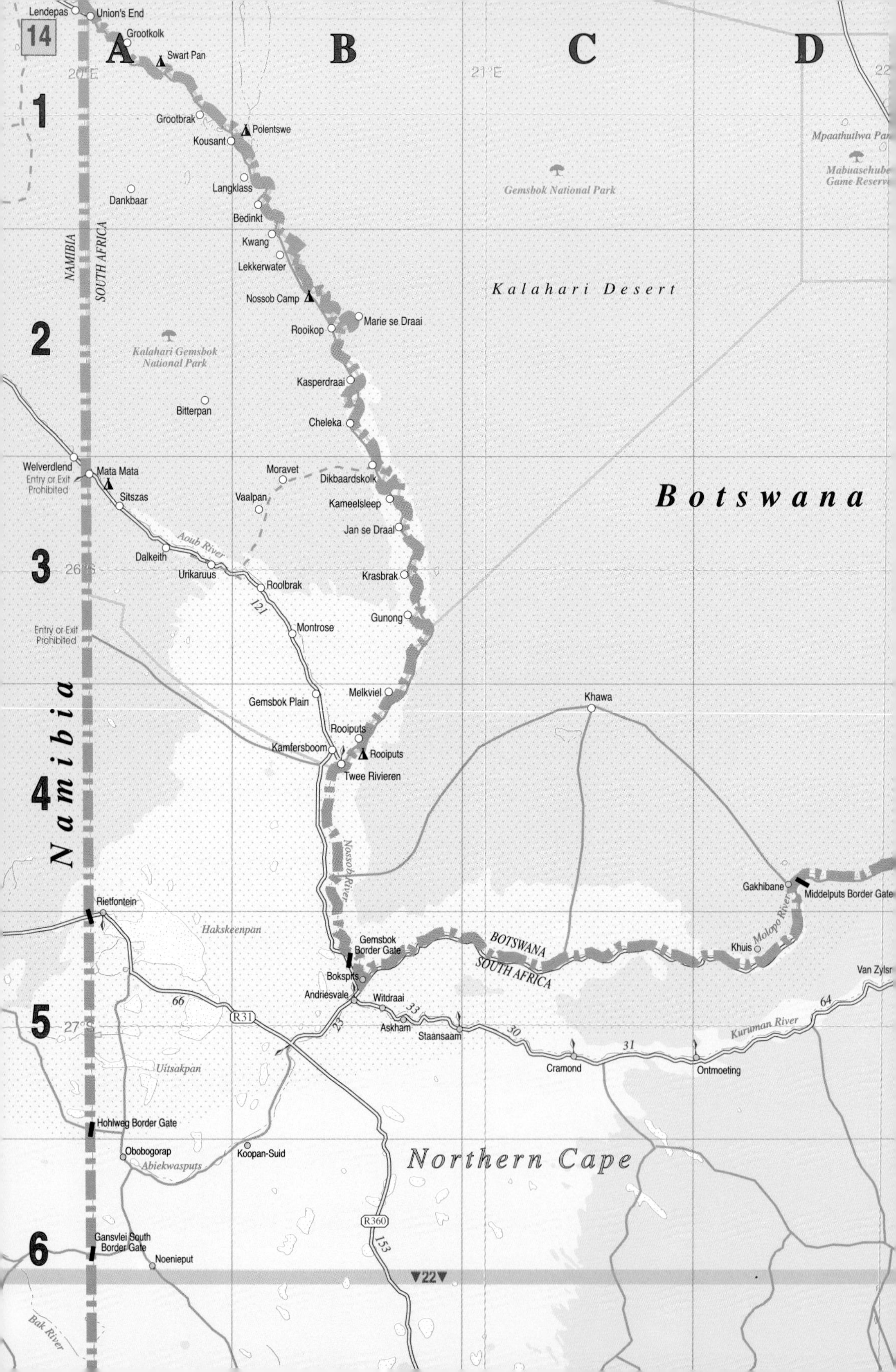
A
B
C
D
1
2
3
4
5
6
20°E
21°E
22
26°S
27°S
Lendepas
Union's End
Grootkolk
Swart Pan
Grootbrak
Polentswe
Kousant
Langklass
Dankbaar
Bedinkt
Kwang
Lekkerwater
Nossob Camp
Marie se Draai
Rooikop
Kasperdraai
Cheleka
Bitterpan
Kalahari Gemsbok National Park
Gemsbok National Park
Mpaathutlwa Pan
Mabuasehube Game Reserve
Kalahari Desert
NAMIBIA
SOUTH AFRICA
Welverdlend
Entry or Exit Prohibited
Mata Mata
Sitszas
Moravet
Vaalpan
Dikbaardskolk
Kameelsleep
Jan se Draai
Botswana
Aoub River
Dalkeith
Urikaruus
Roolbrak
Krasbrak
121
Montrose
Gunong
Entry or Exit Prohibited
Namibia
Gemsbok Plain
Melkviel
Khawa
Rooiputs
Kamfersboom
Rooiputs
Twee Rivieren
Nossob River
Gakhibane
Middelputs Border Gate
Rietfontein
Hakskeenpan
Gemsbok Border Gate
BOTSWANA
SOUTH AFRICA
Khuis
Molopo River
Bokspits
Andriesvale
Witdraai
Van Zylsr
66
R31
23
33
Askham
Staansaam
30
31
64
Kuruman River
Cramond
Ontmoeting
Uitsakpan
Hohlweg Border Gate
Obobogorap
Abiekwasputs
Koopan-Suid
Northern Cape
R360
153
Gansvlei South Border Gate
Noenieput
▼22▼
Bak River

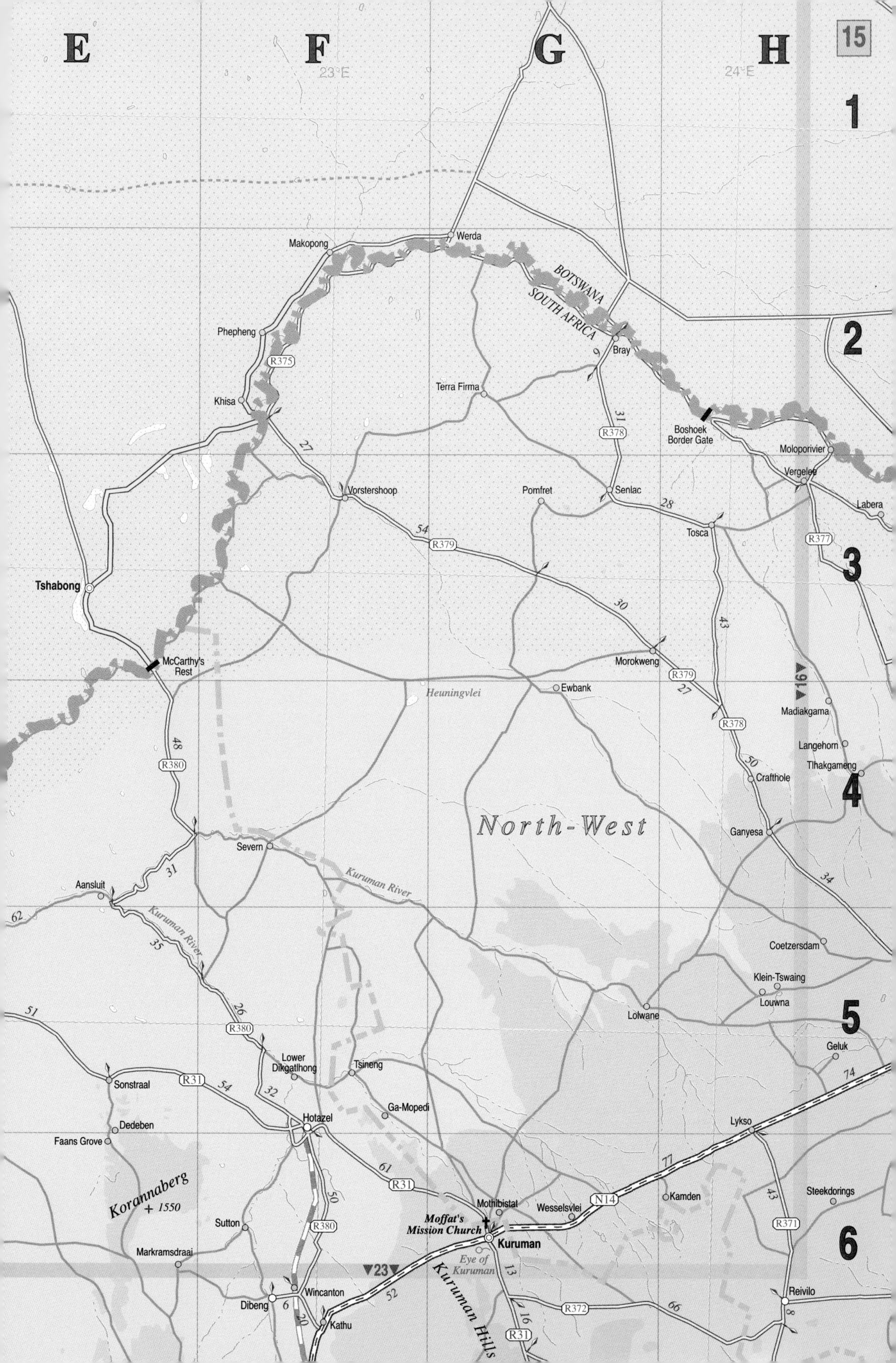
E
F
G
H
23°E
24°E
1
2
3
4
5
6
Werda
Makopong
BOTSWANA
SOUTH AFRICA
Phepheng
R375
Khisa
Bray
Terra Firma
R378
Boshoek
Border Gate
Moloporivier
Vergelee
Labera
Vorstershoop
Pomfret
Senlac
Tosca
R379
R377
Tshabong
Morokweng
McCarthy's
Rest
Heuningvlei
Ewbank
R378
Madiakgama
Langehorn
Tlhakgameng
R380
Crafthole
North-West
Ganyesa
Severn
Aansluit
Kuruman River
Coetzersdam
Klein-Tswaing
Louwna
Lolwane
R380
Geluk
Lower
Dikgatlhong
Tsineng
Sonstraal
R31
Ga-Mopedi
Hotazel
Lykso
Dedeben
Faans Grove
Korannaberg
+ 1550
R31
N14
Kamden
Steekdorings
Mothibistat
Sutton
Moffat's
Mission Church
Wesselsvlei
R380
R371
Kuruman
Markramsdraai
▼23▼
Eye of
Kuruman
Kuruman Hills
Dibeng
Wincanton
Reivilo
R372
Kathu
R31
▼16▼

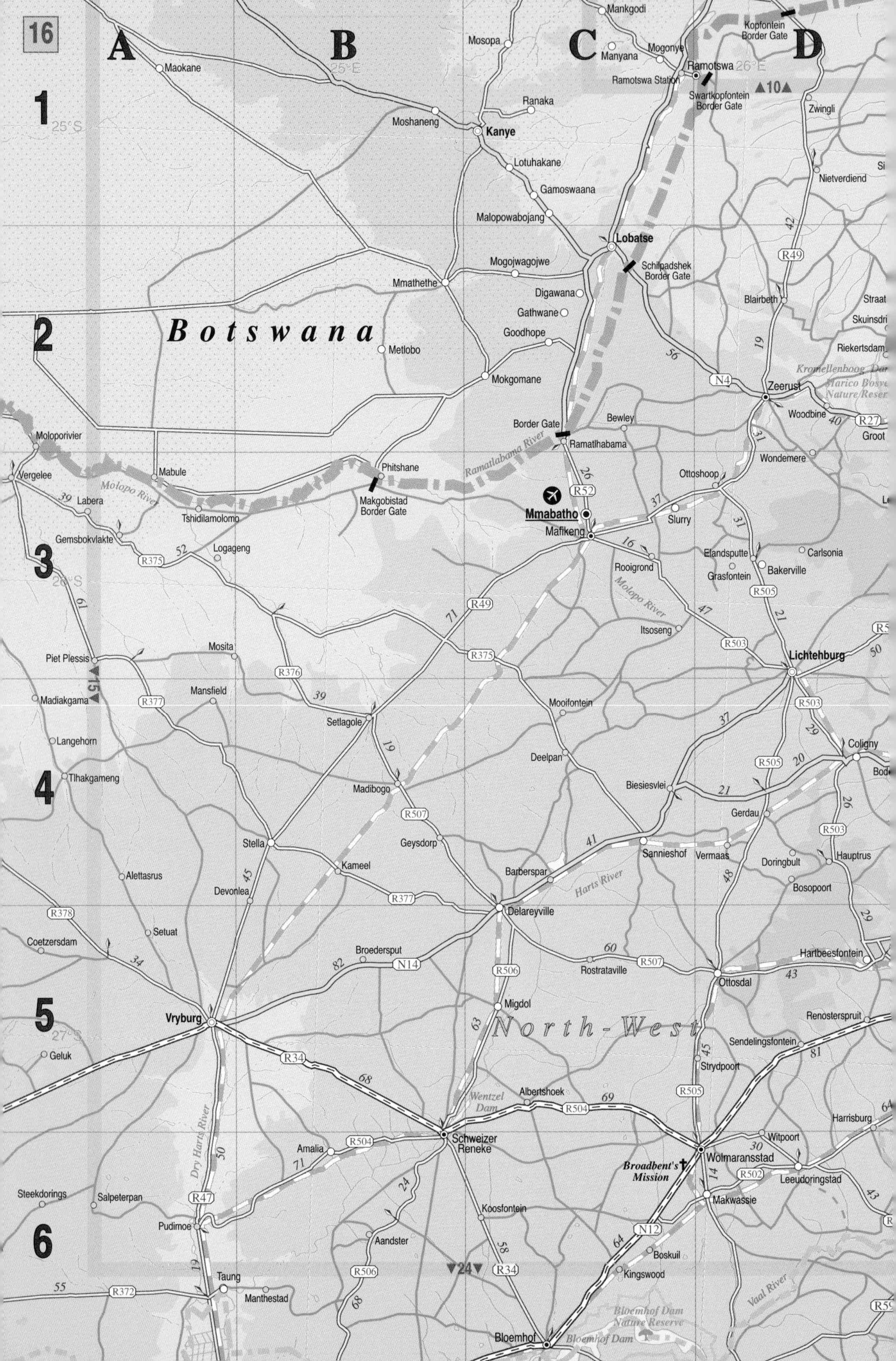

A
B
C
D
1
2
3
4
5
6
Botswana
North-West
Maokane
Mosopa
Mankgodi
Manyana
Mogonye
Ramotswa
Ramotswa Station
Kopfontein Border Gate
Swartkopfontein Border Gate
Zwingli
Ranaka
Moshaneng
Kanye
Lotuhakane
Gamoswaana
Malopowabojang
Nietverdiend
Lobatse
Schilpadshek Border Gate
Mogojwagojwe
Mmathethe
Digawana
Gathwane
Blairbeth
Goodhope
Metlobo
Mokgomane
Zeerust
Kromellenboog Dam
Woodbine
Groot
Border Gate
Ramatlhabama
Bewley
Moloporivier
Vergelee
Mabule
Phitshane
Ramatlabama River
Wondemere
Ottoshoop
Molopo River
Labera
Tshidilamolomo
Makgobistad Border Gate
Mmabatho
Mafikeng
Slurry
Gemsbokvlakte
Logageng
Rooigrond
Elandsputte
Grasfontein
Carlsonia
Bakerville
Itsoseng
Lichtenburg
Mosita
Piet Plessis
Madiakgama
Mansfield
Setlagole
Mooifontein
Langehorn
Coligny
Deelpan
Tlhakgameng
Madibogo
Biesiesvlei
Gerdau
Stella
Geysdorp
Sannieshof
Vermaas
Doringbult
Hauptrus
Alettasrus
Kameel
Barberspar
Harts River
Bosopoort
Devonlea
Delareyville
Coetzersdam
Setuat
Broedersput
Rostrataville
Hartbeesfontein
Ottosdal
Migdol
Vryburg
Renostersspruit
Geluk
Sendelingsfontein
Strydpoort
Albertshoek
Wentzel Dam
Harrisburg
Schweizer Reneke
Witpoort
Amalia
Wolmaransstad
Broadbent's Mission
Leeudoringstad
Dry Harts River
Makwassie
Steekdorings
Salpeterpan
Koosfontein
Pudimoe
Aandster
Boskuil
Kingswood
Taung
Manthestad
Vaal River
Bloemhof Dam Nature Reserve
Bloemhof
Bloemhof Dam
N4
N12
N14
R27
R34
R47
R49
R52
R372
R375
R376
R377
R378
R503
R504
R505
R506
R507
R502
▲10▲
▼24▼
◀15
25°E
26°E
25°S
26°S
27°S

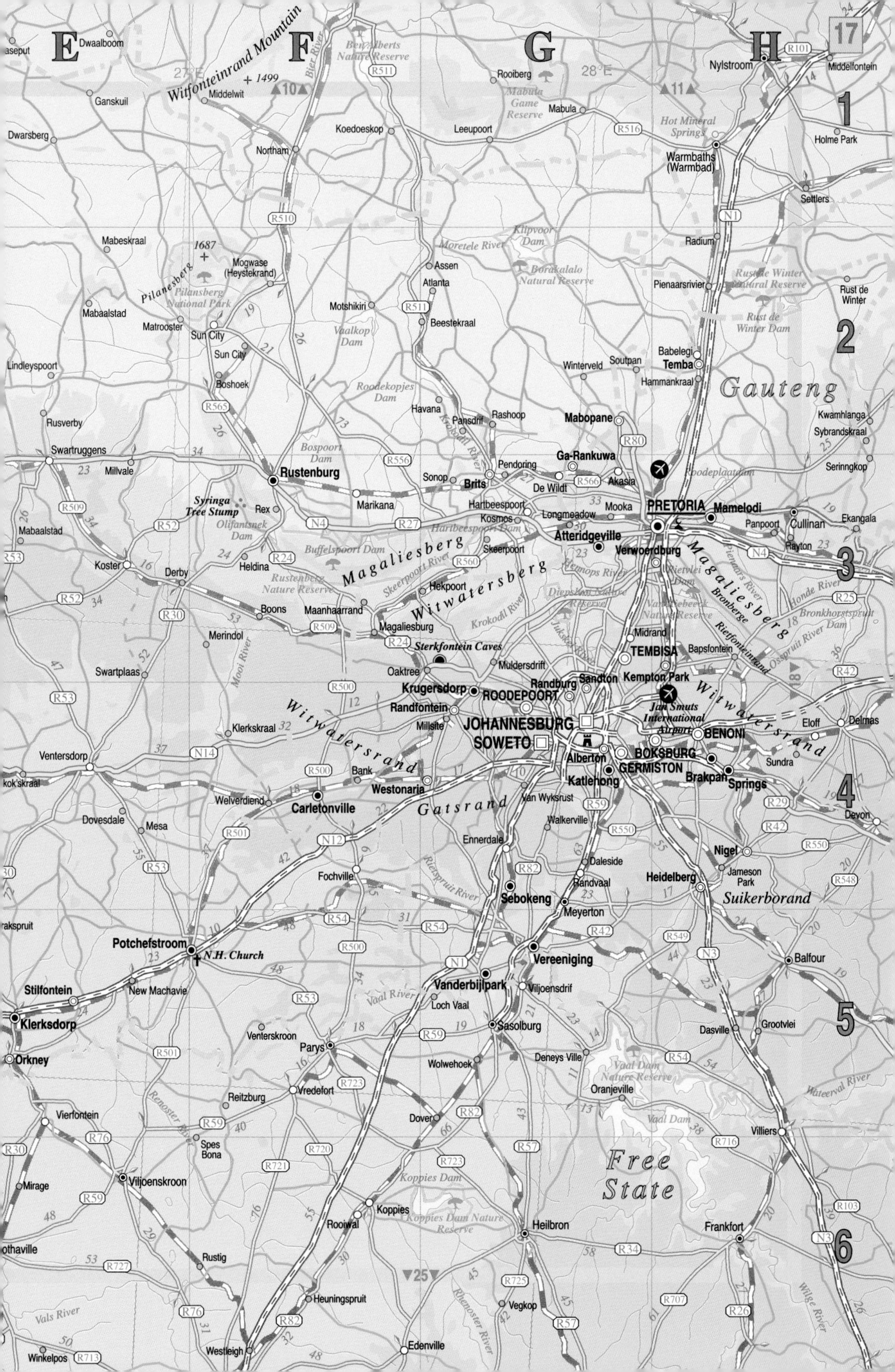
E
F
G
H
1
2
3
4
5
6
27°E
28°E
10
11
25
Dwaalboom
Witfonteinrand Mountain
+ 1499
Middelwit
Ganskuil
Dwarsberg
Northam
Bier River
Ben Alberts Nature Reserve
R511
Rooiberg
Mabula Game Reserve
Mabula
Koedoeskop
Leeupoort
R516
Hot Mineral Springs
Nylstroom
R101
Middelfontein
Holme Park
Warmbaths (Warmbad)
Settlers
N1
Radium
R510
Mabeskraal
1687
Mogwase (Heystekrand)
Pilanesberg
Pilansberg National Park
Mabaalstad
Matrooster
Sun City
Lindleyspoort
Boshoek
R565
Rusverby
Swartruggens
Millvale
Rustenburg
Moretele River
Klipvoor Dam
Assen
Atlanta
Borakalalo Natural Reserve
Motshikiri
R511
Beestekraal
Vaalkop Dam
Roodekopjes Dam
Havana
Pansdrif
Rashoop
Krokodil River
Bospoort Dam
R556
Sonop
Brits
Pendoring
De Wildt
Ga-Rankuwa
R566
Akasia
Mabopane
R80
Winterveld
Soutpan
Babelegi
Temba
Hammankraal
Pienaarsrivier
Rust de Winter Natural Reserve
Rust de Winter
Rust de Winter Dam
Gauteng
Kwamhlanga
Sybrandskraal
Serinngkop
Roodeplaatdam
PRETORIA
Mamelodi
Panpoort
Cullinan
Ekangala
Rayton
N4
Syringa Tree Stump
Rex
Marikana
Hartbeespoort
Kosmos
Hartbeespoort Dam
Longmeadow
Mooka
Olifantsnek Dam
R509
R52
N4
R27
Mabaalstad
R53
Koster
Derby
Heldina
R24
Buffelspoort Dam
Magaliesberg
Skeerpoort
R560
Skeerpoort River
Atteridgeville
Verwoerdburg
Hennops River
Rietvlei Dam
Pienaars River
Bronberge
R25
Honde River
Bronkhorstspruit Dam
Rustenberg Nature Reserve
Hekpoort
Witwatersberg
Diepsloot Nature Reserve
Van Riebeeck Nature Reserve
R52
Boons
Maanhaarrand
R30
R509
Magaliesburg
Krokodil River
Jukskei River
Midrand
Rietfonteinrand
Ossspruit River Dam
Merindol
R24
Sterkfontein Caves
TEMBISA
Bapsfontein
Swartplaas
Mooi River
Muldersdrift
Oaktree
R42
R500
Krugersdorp
ROODEPOORT
Randburg
Sandton
Kempton Park
R53
Randfontein
Jan Smuts International Airport
Witwatersrand
JOHANNESBURG
Millsite
SOWETO
BENONI
Eloff
Delmas
Klerkskraal
N14
Alberton
BOKSBURG
Ventersdorp
Witwatersrand
Bank
GERMISTON
Brakpan
Springs
Sundra
R500
Westonaria
Katlehong
Welverdiend
Carletonville
Gatsrand
Van Wyksrust
R59
R29
Dovesdale
Mesa
R501
N12
Walkerville
R550
R42
Ennerdale
Nigel
R550
Devon
R53
Fochville
R82
Daleside
Rietspruit River
Randvaal
Heidelberg
Jameson Park
R548
Sebokeng
Meyerton
Suikerborand
Potchefstroom
R54
R54
R500
R42
R549
N.H. Church
N1
Vereeniging
N3
Balfour
Stilfontein
New Machavie
R53
Vanderbijlpark
Viljoensdrif
Klerksdorp
Vaal River
Loch Vaal
Sasolburg
Venterskroon
R59
Grootvlei
Dasville
Orkney
R501
Parys
Wolwehoek
Deneys Ville
R54
Vaal Dam Nature Reserve
Reitzburg
R723
Vredefort
Oranjeville
Waterval River
Vierfontein
Renoster River
R59
Dover
R82
Vaal Dam
Villiers
R30
R76
Spes Bona
R720
R57
R723
R716
Mirage
Viljoenskroon
R721
Koppies Dam
Free State
R59
Koppies
Koppies Dam Nature Reserve
Rooiwal
R103
Heilbron
Frankfort
N3
Bothaville
Rustig
R727
R34
R725
Heuningspruit
Rhenoster River
Vegkop
R707
R26
Wilge River
Vals River
R76
R82
R57
Westleigh
Winkelpos
R713
Edenville

18
A
B
C
D
1
2
3
4
5
6
Echo Caves
Roedtan
Crecy
Nylsvley Nature Reserve
29°E
30°E
25°S
26°S
27°S
11
12
17
26
Tompi Seleka
Jane Furse Hospital
Sekhukhune
Aplesdoring
Kromkloof
Burgersfort
Longsight
Steelpoort
Morone
Voortrekkers
Grootboom
Ohrigstad
Mantsibi
Bergpunt
Holme Park
Nutfield
Tuinplaas
Settlers
Glen Cowie
Phokwane
Nebo
Kennedy's Vale
Malaita
Geological Exposure
Marble Hill
Moganyaka
Veraaiersnek Pass
Buffelsvlei
Schalksrus
Waterval Pass
Krugerspos
Graan
Maartenshoop
Vosloosnek
Siyabuswa
Elands River
Hlogotlou
Hereford
Motetema
Steelpoort River
Rust de Winter
Potloodspruit
Gustav Klingbiel Nature Reserve
Bridal Veil Falls
Lone Creek Falls
Lydenburg
Grobersdal
Maleoskop
Erts
Roossenekal
Long Tom Pass
Horseshoe Falls
Witnek
Dennilton
Klipsteen
Driesprong
Voetpad
Bultkop
Rooikraal
Vermont
Asbes
Landsbrook
Loskop Dam Game Reserve
Damwa
Mossiedal
Laersdrif
Kwamhlanga
Sybrandskraal
Loskop Dam
Nederhorst
Strilte
Klipskool
Badfontein
Weltevred
Kwena Dam
Stoffberg
Dullstroom
Goedewil
Kalmoesfontein
Sudwala
Verena
Seringkop
Schoemanskloof Pass
Schoemanskloof
Kwaggaskop
Wilge River
Elands River Valley
Lammerkop
Selonsrivier
Ekangala
Vaalplaas
Fort Merensky
Wonderhoek
Waterval-Boven
Airlie
Bronkhorstspruit
Premier Mine Dam
Kromdraai
Meyersbrug
Mhluzi
Belfast
Machadodorp
Middelburg
Kwaguqa
Balmoral
Wonderfontein
Dalmanutha
Sewefontein
Witbank
Clewer
Klipfontein
Little Olifants River
Nelshoogte Pass
Grobler's-Brug
Arbor
Minnaar
Coalville
Mineral Springs
Badplaas
Ogies
Kendal
Mpumalanga
Delmas
Eloff
Vandyksdrif
Gloria
Carolina
Hendrina
Kriel
Devon
Leandra
Warburton
Breyten
Chrissiesmeer
Kinross
Lundzi Border
Elander
Trichardt
Bethal
Davel
Lothair
Secunda
Ermelo
Lusutfu River
Roodebank
Kaffersspruit
Holbank
Maizefield
Bankkop
Sandlane Nerston Border Gate
Charl Cilliers
Greylingstad
Morgenzon
Sheepmoor
Amsterdam
Val
Nwempisi River
Rock
Holmedene
Bettiesdam
Grootdraai Dam
Vaal River
Waterval River
Panbult
Iswepe
Standerton
Roberts Drift
Meyerville
Free State
Amersfoort
Paltrand
Piet Retief
Anysspruit
Perdekop
Wittenberg
Klip River
Cornelia
Dirkiesdorp
Pongola River
Bergen
Latemanek
Pongola Bush Nature Reserve
Braunschweig
Vrede
Volksrust
Wakkerstroom
Luneberg
Commondale
Charlestown
Balelesberg
N1
N2
N3
N4
N11
N12
N17
R23
R25
R33
R34
R35
R36
R37
R38
R39
R42
R50
R65
R103
R516
R519
R539
R540
R541
R542
R543
R544
R545
R546
R547
R548
R550
R555
R573
R575
R577
R579
R580

E
F
G
H
1
2
3
4
5
6
Mozambique
Swaziland
Indian Ocean
MOZAMBIQUE
SOUTH AFRICA
SWAZILAND
Kruger National Park
Lebombo Mountains
MAPUTO
Mbabane
Manzini
Hhohho
Lubombo
Shiselweni
Mbutini Hills
Bulungu
Mahlangatsha
Magude
Xinavane
Manhiça
Marracuene
Moamba
Matola
Boane
Namaacha
Komatipoort
Ressano Garcia
Lebombo Border Gate
Bela Vista
Salamanga
Ponta do Ouro
Maputo Elephant Reserve
Ndumu Game Reserve
Tembe Elephant Reserve
Kosi Bay Nature Reserve
Maputaland Marine Reserve
Louis Trichardttrek Memorial
Trichardt Memorial
Lindanda Memorial
Sabie Sand Private Game Reserve
Inyati Game Reserve
Hlane Royal National Park
Mkhaya Game Reserve
Milwane Wildlife Sanctuary
Mlawula Nature Reserve
Malolotja Nature Reserve
Phophonyane Falls
Rock Paintings
Mission Falls
Sigombeni Falls
Mbuluzi Falls
Cecil Macks Pass
Mpageni Pass
Saddleback Pass
Lomahasha Border Gate
Mananga Border Gate
Matsam Border Gate
Goba Fronteira Border Closed
Onverwacht Border Gate
Nelspruit
Barberton
Hazyview
Bosbokrand
Skukuza
Lavumisa
Big Bend
Siteki
Piggs Peak
Bulembu
Nhlangano
Ingwavuma
Ndumo
Inhaca
Cabo de Santa Maria
Ponta de Macaneta
Ponta Milibangalala
▲12▲
▼27▼

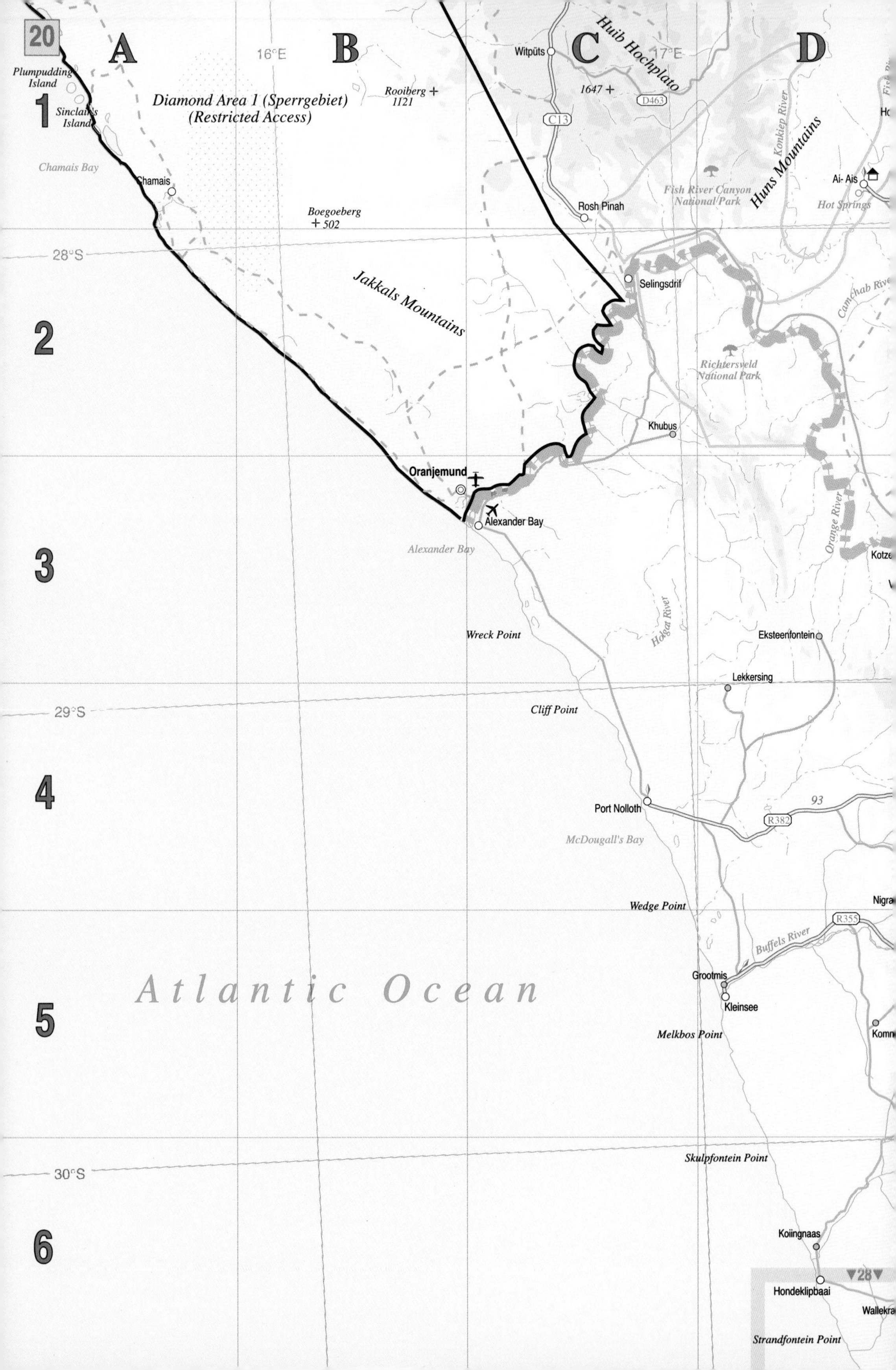
20
A
B
C
D
16°E
17°E
1
2
3
4
5
6
28°S
29°S
30°S
Plumpudding Island
Sinclair's Island
Chamais Bay
Chamais
Diamond Area 1 (Sperrgebiet) (Restricted Access)
Rooiberg 1121
Boegoeberg 502
Jakkals Mountains
Witpüts
Huib Hochplato
1647
D463
C13
Rosh Pinah
Konkiep River
Huns Mountains
Fish River Canyon National Park
Ai-Ais
Hot Springs
Selingsdrif
Camchab River
Richtersveld National Park
Khubus
Oranjemund
Alexander Bay
Orange River
Kotze
Wreck Point
Holgat River
Eksteenfontein
Lekkersing
Cliff Point
Port Nolloth
93
R382
McDougall's Bay
Wedge Point
Nigra
R355
Buffels River
Grootmis
Kleinsee
Melkbos Point
Komm
Atlantic Ocean
Skulpfontein Point
Koiingnaas
28
Hondeklipbaai
Wallekra
Strandfontein Point

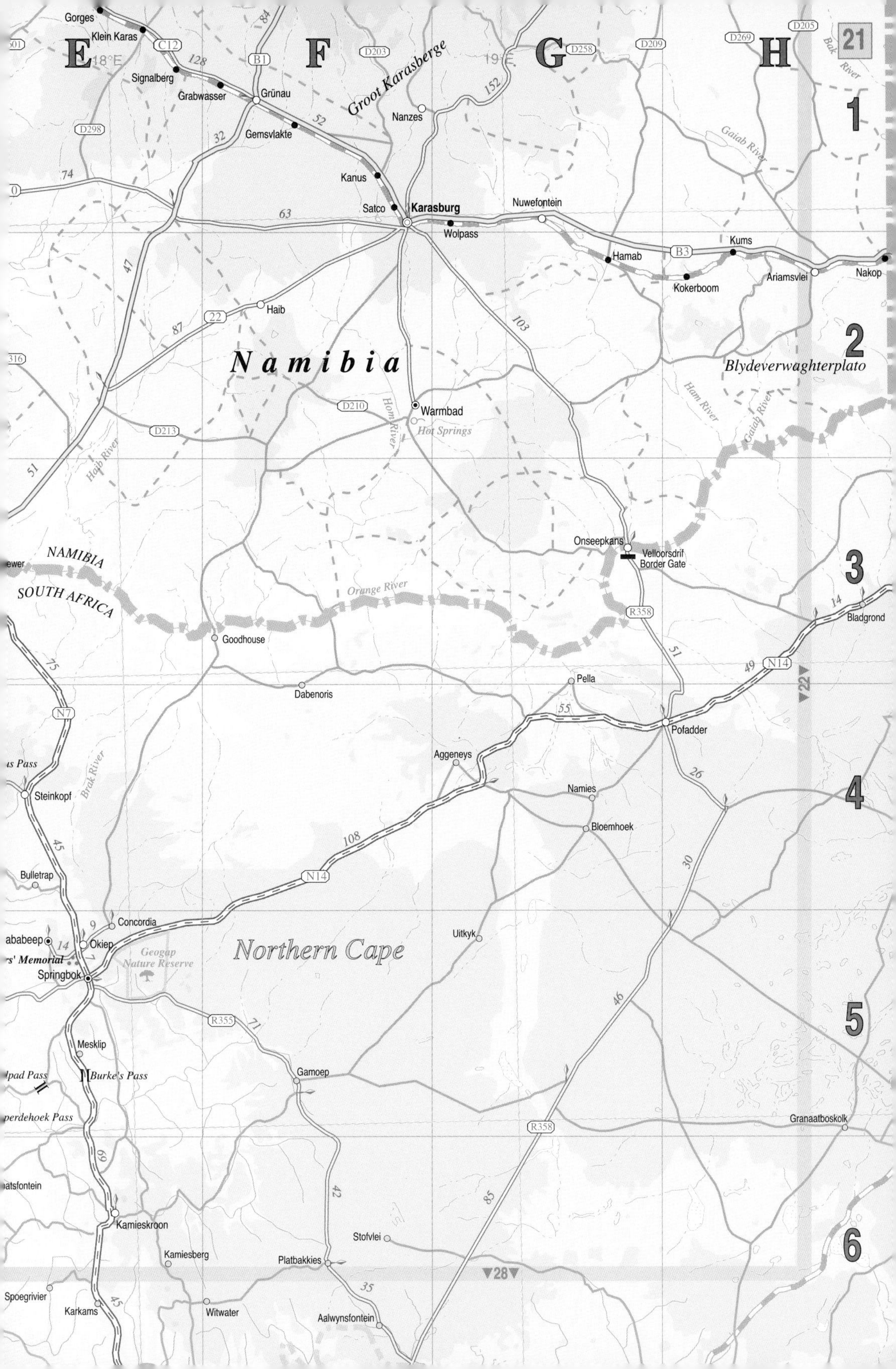
E
F
G
H
1
2
3
4
5
6
Namibia
NAMIBIA
SOUTH AFRICA
Northern Cape
Groot Karasberge
Blydeverwaghterplato
Orange River
Gorges
Klein Karas
Signalberg
Grabwasser
Grünau
Gemsvlakte
Nanzes
Kanus
Satco
Karasburg
Wolpass
Nuwefontein
Hamab
Kums
Kokerboom
Ariamsvlei
Nakop
Haib
Warmbad
Hot Springs
Onseepkans
Velloorsdrif Border Gate
Goodhouse
Dabenoris
Pella
Pofadder
Bladgrond
Aggeneys
Namies
Bloemhoek
Steinkopf
Bulletrap
Concordia
Okiep
Springbok
Geogap Nature Reserve
Uitkyk
Mesklip
Burke's Pass
Gamoep
Granaatboskolk
Kamieskroon
Kamiesberg
Stofvlei
Platbakkies
Spoegrivier
Karkams
Witwater
Aalwynsfontein
Haib River
Hom River
Ham River
Gaiab River
Brak River
Bak River
C12
B1
B3
N7
N14
R355
R358
D203
D258
D209
D269
D205
D298
D210
D213
22
▼22▼
▼28▼

A
B
C
D
1
2
3
4
5
6
20°E
21°E
22°
28°S
29°S
30°S
▲14▲
▼21▼
▼29▼
NAMIBIA
SOUTH AFRICA
Bak River
Vrouenspan
Bokhara
R360
Swartmodder
Harrisdale
Nakop
N10
Ariamsvlei
Grondneus
Gelukspruit
Langklip
132
Blydeverwaghterplato
Spitskop Nature Reserve
42
N14
Lutzputs
Upington
Dagbreek
Karos
85
Augrabies Falls
Augrabies Falls National Park
Louisvale
39
Grootdrink
Kalkwerf
Augrabies
Kanoneiland
28
Marchand
Keimos
50
40
Alheit
Kakamas
R359
Neilersdrif
44
21
Orange River
Wegdraai
18
N14
Nabies
64
14
Bladgrond
Skerpioenp
14
Groblershoop
Kleinbegin
R27
85
Sout River
Harrebeest River
Koegrabie
25
Putsonderwater
71
R383
37
Kenhardt
Draghoe
Bossiekom
Tuins River
Rooiberg Dam
Maryo
Northern Cape
Jaght Drift
148
79
R361
Diemansputs
Karreeboschkolk
Grootvloer
Verneuk Pan
Granaatboskolk
Halfweg
Zwartkop
68
Onderstedorings
R27
Van Wyksvlei
59
30
61
Brandvlei

E
F
G
H
1
2
3
4
5
6
Wincanton
Dibeng
Kathu
N14
Sishen
Dingle
Moeswal
Langkloof Pass
Olifantshoek
Vroeggedeel
Lohatlha
R386
R385
Postmasburg
Langberg
Bermolli
Matsap
Volop
N8
Griekwastad
Asbesberge
Koegelbeen Caves
Campbell
Livingstone Church
Kuruman Hills
R31
R372
R373
Bekker
Blikfontein
Reivilo
Blesmanspos
Madipelesa
Boetsap
Wonderwerk Caves
Danielskuil
Swartputs
Owendale
Koopmansfontein
Lime Acres
Silver Streams
Papkuil
R370
Ulco
Delportshoop
Sidney On Vaal
Longlands
Vaal River
Vaalbos National Park
Schmidtsdrif
R357
Koedoesberg
Douglas
Bucklands
Plooysburg
R383
Westerberg
Koegas
Nieketkshoop
Higg's Hope
R357
Salt Lake
N12
Graspan
Belmont
Witput
Wanda
Old Wagon Bridge
Hopetown
Oranjerivier
Orange River
Orania
R369
R388
Kraankuil
R387
Fransenhof
Prieska
Prieskapoort Pass
Strydenburg
N10
Omdraaisvlei
Sodium
R403
R386
Poupan
Potfontein
Houtwater Dam
Houtkraal
Philipstown
R48

A
B
C
D
1
2
3
4
5
6
Taung
Manthestad
Bloemhof
Bloemhof Dam Nature Reserve
Bloemhof Dam
Vaal River
25°E
26°E
Hartswater
Pampierstad
Sandveld Nature Reserve
Madipelesa
Rock Engravings
Mineral Springs
Hoopstad
Wessels
Boetsap
Espagsdrif
Jan Kempdorp
Christiana
Ganspan
28°S
Harts River
Tierfontein
Warrenton
Hertzogville
Mount Rupert
Vaalharts Dam
Content
Northern Cape
Bultfontein
Delportshoop
Windsorton
Windsorton Road
Sidney On Vaal
Longlands
Vaalbos National Park
Barkly West
Riverton
Volkspele Monument
Boshof
Archaeological Reserve
Kenilworth
Big Hole
Dealesville
Soutpan
Brandfort
KIMBERLEY
Florisbad
Spytfontein
Magersfontein
Paardeberg
Soetdoring Nature Reserve
Karee
Modder River
Wolwespruit
Koedoesberg
Krugerdrif Dam
29°S
Ritchie
Modderrivier
Petrusburg
Glen
Jacobsdal
De Brug
BLOEMFONTEIN
Heuningneskloof
Shannon
Mangaung
Sannasp
Free State
Ferreira
Rodenbeck
Graspan
Riet River
Rustfontein Nature Res
Rustfontein
Belmont
Koffiefontein
Tierpoort
Kalkfontein Dam Nature Reserve
Rooipan
Riet River
Wanda
Austin's Post
Kalkfontein Dam
Dewe
Reddersburg
Luckhoff
Jagersfontein
Fauresmith
Edenburg
Wolvepoort
Krugers
30°S
Vanderkloof
Reebokrand
Trompsburg
Gomvlei
Petrusville
Breipaal
Vanderkloof Dam
Philippolis Road
Lofter
Philippolis
Springfontein
Smith
Waterkloof
Dupleston
Philipstown
Orange River
Tussen die Riviere Game Farm
Priors
Caledon R

E
F
G
H
1
2
3
4
5
6
Vals River
Heuningspruit
Vegkop
Rhenoster River
Wilge River
27°E
28°E
Winkelpos
Westleigh
Edenville
17
Tweeling
Maokeng
Kroonstad
Petrus Steyn
Allanridge
Prehistoric Stone Huts
Odendaalsrus
Geneva
Wonderkop
Reitz
Riebeeckstad
Alma
Thabong
Welkom
Hennenman
Steynsrus
Lindley
Molen River
Whites
Virginia
Ventersburg
Arlington
Danielsrus
Liebenbergs River
Welgelee
Libertas
Sand River
Valsrivier
Kransfontein
Willem Pretorius Nature Reserve
Theron
Allemanskraal Dam
Bohlakong
Bethlehem
Aberfeldy
Saulspoort Dam
Senekal
Paul Roux
Pretoriuskloof Nature Reserve
Theunissen
Kestell
Erfenis Nature Reserve
Erfenis Dam
Winburg
Witteberg
Noupoortsnek Pass
Rooiberg
Rosendal
Clarens
2477
QwaQwa Conservation Area
Golden Gate Highlands National Park
Phuthaditjhaba
Marquard
Fouriesburg
Libono Camp
Sefako
Hendrick's Drift
Qholaqhoe
Rusder's Valley
Caledonspoort Border Gate
Joel's Drift
Khatibe
Oxbow
Royal Natal National Park
Moteng
Malibamatso River
Verkeerdevliei
Butha-Buthe
Moteng Pass
Witsieshoek Mountain
Mount-Aux-Sources
3282
Allandale
Gumtree
Ficksburg
Jonathane
Khabo
Butha-Buthe
Excelsior
Clocolan
Ficksburg Border Gate
Maputsoe
Leribe (Hlotse)
Malaoaneng
Pela-Tsoeu
Peka Bridge Border Gate
Peka
Corn Exchange
Mahobong
Matlameng
Mekoatleng Pass
Lemphane
Pitseng
3277
Liqhobong
Mothae
Kolonyama
Koeneng
Rampai's Pass
Kao Mine
Letseng-la-Terae
Phutiatsana River
Rakoloi
Mamathe
Mapoteng
Tweespruit
Westminster
Leribe
Pelaneng
Thaba 'Nchu
Marseilles
Ladybrand
Caledon River
Tebetebeng
Nokong
Ha Lejone
Moletsane
Maluti Mountains
Teya-Teyaneng
Mokhotlong
Mateka
Sefikeng
Katse Reservoir
Seshote
Mapholaneng
Maria Moroka National Park
Kommissiepoort
Maseru Bridge Border Gate
Moshoeshoe's Mountain Fortress
Berea
Methalaneng
St Martin
Tlokoeng
Khatleli
Leeurivier Dam
MASERU
Ha Baroana
Thaba Bosiu
Malingoaneng
Glenrock
Bushman's Pass
Bokong
Masianokeng
Katse
Makhuleng
Mazenod
Matela
Mpaoo
Machache
God Help Me Pass
Central Range
Rafolatsane
Sengu River
Blue Mountain Pass
Roma
Molimo-Nthuse
Jordane
Molumong
Mokhalinyane
Thot'a-Moli
Likalaneng
Hobhouse
Makhaleng
Cheche Pass
Linakaneng
Caledon River
Kolo
Mofoka
Tlali
Ngope Ts'oeu
Marakabei
Mokhoabong Pass
Linakeng
Palama
Matsieng
Maseru
Mantsonyane
Thaba-Tseka
Taung Ha Makunyapane
Linakeng River
Jammersdrif
TsaKholo
Morija
Thaba Phats'oa
Van Rooyen's Gate
Raleqheka
Ramabanta
Mashai River
Wepener
Tebang
Thaba Putsoa
Thaba-Tseka
Litsoetse
Mashai
Caledon Nature Reserve
Letsunyane
Thaba Putsoa 3096
Mosala
Makhakhe
Lesobeng River
Likupa
Sehonghong
Mafeteng
Mafeteng
Rock Paintings
Semonkong
Welbedacht Dam
Boranta
Ketane Falls
Thetsane
Maletsunyane Falls
Matelile
Malealea
Matebeng
Matebeng Pass
Khobotle
Qaba
Lesotho
Sephapo's Border Gate
Thabana-Morena
Matsaile
Vanstadensrus
Makhaleng River
Maletsunyane River
Qacha's Nek
Leqooa
Paulus
Boesmanskop
Egmont Dam
Ts'Oloane
Mpharane
Sekake
Cannibal Caves
Sebili
Nohana
Mokopung
Tsoelike
Tsoelike River
Kubung
Qobong
Makhalengburg Border Gate
Mohale's Hoek
Mahlakaneng
Mpiti
Quthing
32
Chief Moorosi's Mountain Fortress
Senqu River
Qacha's Nek
Mohale's Hoek
Mekaling
Mt Moorosi
Mphaki
Mount Moorosi
2356
Mafube
Lehlohonolo
Zastron
Fort Hartley
Mosehle
Ongeluksnek Border Gate
Roamer's Rest
Rouxville
Phatlalla
Tosing
Lethena
26
R76
R82
R34
R713
R725
R707
R57
R26
R714
N1
R73
N5
R707
R708
R709
R703
A1
N6
A3
A5
A2
R20
A4

A
B
C
D
1
2
3
4
5
6
Vrede
Volksrust
Charlestown
Wakkerstroom
Braunschweig
Pongola River
Pongola Bush Nature Reserve
Commondale
Balelesberg
Groenvlei
Paulpietersburg
Grootspruit
Laing's Nek
18
Ingogo
Rietkuil
Seekoeivlei Nature Reserve
Bothas Pass
Memel
Bivane
Mpemvana
Hot Sp
Utrecht
Zungwini
Newcastle
Madadeni
Warden
Free State
Molen River
Mullers Pass
Ballengeich
Osizweni
Vryheid
Scheepersnek
Verkykerskop
Mont Pelaan
Bloedrivier
Chelmsford Dam
Chelmsford Dam Nature Reserve
Normandien
Dannhauser
Kingsley
Calvert
Hattingspruit
Ntabebomvu
Aberfeldy
Blood River Monument
Fort Mistake
Dundee
Glencoe
Van Rooyen
Blood River
Bushman Paintings
Cundycleugh
Harrismith
De Beers Pass
Biggarsberg
Nondweni
Vant's Drift
Nqutu
Swinburne
Van Reenen
Craigsforth
Wasbank
Sterkfontein Dam Nature Reserve
Driefontein
Rorke's Drift
Wyford
Phuthaditjhaba
Sterkfontein Dam
Van Reenen Pass
Besters
Elandslaagte
Isandlwana
Silutshana
QwaQwa Conservation Area
Geluksburg
Pepworth
Sundays River
Helpmekaar
2329
Sand River Valley
Elandskraal
Babangiboni
Olivieshoek Pass
Ladysmith
Mangeni
KwaZulu/Natal
Pomeroy
Witsieshoek Mountain
Spioenkop Nature Reserve
Rossboom
Royal Natal National Park
Spioenkop Dam
Tugela Heights Battlefield
Qudeni
3282
Mount-Aux-Sources
Bergville
Colenso
25
Woodstock Dam
Tugela River
Letseng-la-Terae
Winterton
Tugela Ferry
Dlolwana
Chieveley
Zunckels
Weenen
Mothae
Cleft Peak 3261
Frere
Weenen Nature Reserve
Keate's Drift
Letseng-la-Terae
Loskop
Bloukrans Monument
The Ranch
Cathedral Peak 3004
Cathedral Peak State Forest
Estcourt
Muden
Kathkin Peak 3181
Wagendrift Dam
Kranskop
Drakensberg
Mooi River
Champagne Castle 3377
Ntabamhlope
Wagendrift Nature Reserve
Greytown
Craigie Burn Dam
Ahrens
Motsitseng
Mafadi 3450
Kwa Sizaba Mission
Tlokoeng
Khatleli
Giant's Castle Game Reserve
Rockmount
South Downs
Fort Mtombeni
Mokhotlong
Mooi River
Rietvlei
Sevenoaks
Giant's Castle
Molumong
Rafolatsane
Rosetta
Highmoor State Forest
Redcliffe
Umvoti River
Giants Castle 3312
Matsoaning
Lesotho
Kambery
Nottingham Road
Kamberg Nature Reserve
York
New Hanover
Dalton
The Natal Drakensberg Park
Albert Falls Nature Reserve
Fawnleas
Thabana-Ntlenyana 3481
Redi 3298
Balgowan
Mpolweni
Masenkeng
Loteni Nature Reserve
Lidgetton
Mkhomazi State Forest
Dargle
Albert Falls
Cobham State Forest
Howick
Wartburg
Lower Loteni
Umgeni Valley Nature Reserve
Midmar Public Nature Reserve
Sani Top
Sani Pass Border Gate
Sani Pass
Merrivale
Valley of 1000 Hills
Midmar Dam
Queen Elizabeth Park
Mpendle
Hilton
Ndwedwe
PIETERMARITZBURG
Drakensberg
Edendale
Tongaat
Bushman's Nek & Border Post
Himeville Nature Reserve
Ashburton
Himeville
Verulam
Matebeng Pass
Garden Castle State Forest
Umdloti
Camperdown
Mgeni River
Inanda
Underberg
Thornville
Bulwer
Mpumalanga
Phoenix
Leqooa
Sehlabathebe
KwaMashu
Paulus
Sehlabathebe National Park
Hammarsdale
Clermont
Coleford Nature Reserve
Pinetown
Richmond
Donnybrook
Nshongweni Dam
DURB
Moshebi
Queensburg
Kingscote
Coleford
Rosebank
Kenneth Stainbank National Park
The Bluf
Creighton
Umlazi
Riverside
33
Umbumbulu
Isipingo
Mzimkulu River
Lovu River
Umbogintwini
Adams Mission
Lehlohonolo
Kingsburgh
Amanzimtoti
Ixopo
Mkomazi River
Swartberg
New Amalfi
Sneezewood
Umgababa
N3
N11
N2
R34
R543
R722
R33
R68
R621
R602
R712
R74
R616
R600
R622
R617
R56
R624
R603
R612
2277

E
F
G
H
1
2
3
4
5
6
32°E
33°E
Berbice
Mhlosheni
Hluthi
Ingwavuma
Onverwacht Border Gate
Sitilo River
Lavumisa
Golela
Pongola
Pongola River
Maputaland Marine Reserve
Pongolapoort Dam
Pongolapoort Public Resort Nature Reserve
Lake Sibaya
Lake Sibaya Nature Reserve
Hully Point
Sodwana Bay
Itala Game Reserve
Louwsburg
Magudu
Candover
Jozini
Mbaswana
Jesser Point
Sodwana Bay National Park
Ubombo
Mahlangasi
Mkuze
Mkuze River
529
Ghost Mountain
Mkuzi Game Reserve
Greater St Lucia Wetlands
Steilrand
Ngome
Msinduzi River
Phinda Resource Reserve
St Lucia Park & Game Reserve
Swart Umfolozi
Nongoma
False Bay Park
Leven Point
Lake St Lucia
Hluhluwe
Nhlazatsshe
Hlabisa
Hluhluwe Dam
Cape Vidal
Tewati Wilderness Area
Fort Nolela
Mahlabatini
Black Umfolozi River
Corridor Reserve
Ulundi
Somkele
Hluluwe-Umfolozi Park
White Mfolozi River
Mtonjaneni
St Lucia
Mtubatuba
Dukuduku Forest Reserve
Riverview
Melmoth
Osborn
Cape St Lucia
Teza
Red Hill
175
Ndundulu
Kwa-Mbonambi
Nkwalini
Enselent Nature Reserve
Mposa
Mzingazi Lake
Nsezi Lake
Empangeni
Entumeni Nature Reserve
Coward's Bush Monument
Richards Bay
Felixton
Mhlatuzi Lagoon
Entumeni
Eshowe
Fort Kwa-Mondi
Richards Bay Game Reserve
Uqupa Lake
Nongqai Fort
Umlalazi Nature Reserve
Mtunzini
Gingindlovu
Amatikulu
Nyoni
Mandini
Tugela
Battle of the Tugela
Newark
Tugela Mouth
Fort Pearson
Darnall
Shaka's Memorial
Zinkwazi
Blythdale
Sheffield Beach
Indian Ocean
R66
R69
R618
R34
N2
19

28
A
B
C
D
1
2
3
4
5
6
Hondeklipbaai
Wallekraal
Spoegrivier
Karkams
Witwater
Aalwynsfontein
Strandfontein Point
18°E
19°E
▲20▲
▲21▲
Garies
Kliprand
1024
R355
R358
Bokkeveldberg
Sout River
Nariep
Groen River
Swartdoorn River
875
Groenriviersmond
Island Point
Kotzesrus
Biesiesfontein
Rietpoort
Loeriesfontein
31°S
Bitterfontein
Nuwerus
R357
Konikans
Sout River
Brandkop
R363
Landplaas
Nieuwoudtville
Nieuwoudtville Wild Flower Reserve
Vanrhyns Pass
Grootdrif
Oorlogskloof Nature Reserve
Koekenaap
Lutzville
N7
R27
Olifants River
Vanrhynsdorp
R362
R364
Vredendal
Oorlogskloof River
Papendorp
Botterkloof
Spruitdrif
Klawer
Strandfontein
Doring Bay
Trawal
Doringbos
Heerenlogement Cave
Rooiduine Point
Heerenlogement
Ratelfontein
32°S
Uitspankraal
Lambert's Bay
Clanwilliam
Pakhuis Pass
Wolfhuis
Graafwater
Leipoldtville
Clanwilliam Dam
Cederberg
Wuppertal
Eland's Bay
Sandberg
Baboon Point
Algeria
2027
Redelinghuys
Atlantic Ocean
R366
Cederberg Wilderness Area
Paleisheuwel
Ndoordkuil
Cederberg
Het Kruis
Citrusdal
Piekenaarskloof
Middelberg Pass
St Helena Bay
Dwarskersbos
Aurora
Eendekuil
Stompneus Point
Western Cape
Stompneusbaai
St Helena Bay
Laaiplek
Paternoster
Velddrif
Pools
Bokfontein
Cape Columbine
Columbine National Reserve
R399
Goedverwag
Sauer
R365
Piketberg
Vredenburg
Piketberg
Bergrivier
Witwater
R44
De Hoek
R303
Great Berg
Saldanha
33°S
R45
Koringberg
Porterville
Groot Winterhoek Wilderness Area
Saldanha Bay
Hopefield
Plankies Bay
Langebaan
▼34▼
2078
Groot Winterhoek
Moorreesburg
Postberg National Reserve
Churchhaven
Saronberg
1800
Gydo
West Coast National Park
Rust
R311
Tulbagh
Prince Alfred Hamlet
R45
Gouda

E
F
G
H
1
2
3
4
5
6
Brandvlei
Van Wyksvlei
20°E
21°E
Riet Se Vloer
Rock Paintings
Swartkolkvloer
Tontelbos
Sakrivier
Corbelled Houses
Sak River
Kootjieskolk
Doring River
Williston
Sterling
1673 + Hantamsberg
Calvinia
Northern Cape
Riet River
Quaggasfontein Poort
Bloukrans Pass
Saaifontein
Corbelled House
Bonekraal
Fish River
Middelpos
Fraserburg
Die Bos
Snyderspoort
Renoster River
Bastersberge
The Karoo
Roggeveldberge
Teekloof Pass
1913
Hondefontein
Tankwa Karoo National Park
Sutherland
Nuweveldberge
Bo Wadrif
Rooikloof
Tankwa River
Verlatekloof
Komsberge
1721
Komsberg Pass
Merweville
Koringplaas
Buffels River
Kruidfontein
Zwarts
Prince Albert Road
Dwyka
Hillandale
Koup
Vleifontein
Laingsburg
Baviaan
Matjiesfontein
Pieter Meintjies
Die Venster
Verkeerdevlei Dam
Witteberge
Paradehoek
+1474
Rooinek
Floriskraal Dam
Gamkapoort Dam
Dwyka River
Gamka River
Bosluiskloof
R353
R357
R27
R63
R355
R354
R356
R361
R328
N1
▼21▼
▼22▼
▼30▼
▼34▼
▼35▼

30
A
B
C
D
1
2
3
4
5
6
Van Wyksvlei
Houtwater Dam
Bushman Drawings
▲23▲
Vosburg
Giesenskraal
Britstown
Kareeberge
Volstruispoort
Smartt Syndicate Dam
Groen River
Kareebospoort
Carnarvon
Pampoenpoort
Dieput
Mynfontein
Deelfontein
Stekaar
Merriman
De Klerk
Northern Cape
Brakpoort
Ongers River
Victoria West
Richmond
Loxton
Meltonwold
Hutchinson
Verster
Saaifontein
Biesiespoort
▼29▼
Wagenaarskraal
Sneeukraal
Three Sisters
Murraysburg
Rosedene
Western Cape
Restvale
Nelspoort
Molteno Pass
Renosterkop
Roseseberg Pass
Karoo National Park
Beaufort West
Droërivier
Kariega River
Salt River
Aberdeen
Letjiesbos
Leeuw
Leeu Gamka Dam
Luttig
Wiegnaarspoort
Leeu Gamka
Kaapse Poortjie
Kruidfontein
Zwarts
Rietbron
Salt River
Beervlei Dam
Seekoegat
Miller
Volstruisleegte
Swanepoelspoort
Kommandokraal
Witteberge
▼35▼
▼36▼
Groot River
Prince Albert
Oukloof Dam
Perdepoort
Swartberg Pass
Klaarstroom
Willowmore
R386
R384
R361
R63
R403
R398
R388
N12
R356
R381
N1
R353
R332
R61
N9
R328
R407
R337
R329
22°E
23°E
24°E
31°S
32°S
33°S
1511
1450
1414

E
F
G
H
1
2
3
4
5
6
Philipstown
Colesberg
Noupoort
Middelburg
Hanover
Burgersdorp
Steynsburg
Molteno
Sterkstroom
Hofmeyr
Cradock
Tarkastad
Graaff Reinet
Pearston
Somerset East
Cookhouse
Bedford
Adelaide
Fort Beaufort
Jansenville
Klipplaat
Bethulie
Venterstad
Oviston
Eastern Cape
Sneeuberg
Bankberg
Bamboesberg
Winterberg
Mountain Zebra National Park
Karoo Nature Reserve
Gariep Nature Reserve
Tussen die Riviere Game Farm
Tsolwana Game Reserve
Taal Monument
Lootsberg Pass
Naudesberg Pass
Wapadsberg Pass
Swaershoek Pass
Daggaboersnek
Soutpansnek
Ecca Pass
Fort Brown

A
B
C
D
1
2
3
4
5
6
Mohale'shoek
Chief Moorosi's Mountain Fortress
Mt Moorosi
Mount Moorosi 2356
Mphaki
Lethena
Roamer's
Ongeluksnek Border Gate
Thaba Chitja
Tosing
Ralebona
Rock Paintings
Mosehle
Fort Hartley
Mekaling
Phatlalla
Alwynskop
Palmietfontein
Telebrug Border Gate
Quthing (Moyeni)
Quthing
Muruloane River
Kinirapoort
Zastron
Rouxville
Goedemoed
Orange River
Bluegums
Sterkspruit
Herschel
Hot Sulphur Springs
Aliwal North
Lady Grey
Avoca Peak 2769
Lundean's Nek
Ben Macdhui 3001
Karringmelkspruit
New England
Rhodes
Naudesnek
Elands Height
Pitseng Pass
Lower Pitseng
Mount Fletcher
Tina River
Lahlangubo
Moshesh's Ford
Barkly East
Moordenaarsnek
Katkop
Vineyard
Clanville
Halcyon Drift
Tsisana River
Witkop
Jamestown
Clifford
Triple Streams
Maclear
Swempoort
Mooi River
Rossouw
Barkly Pass
Ugie
Ntywenka
Bushman Paintings and Caves
Morristown
Eastern Cape
Stormberg
Penhoek Pass
2127
Dordrecht
Elliot
Syfergat
Boesmanshoek Pass
Sterkstroom
Cala Road
Ida
Xalanga
Quiba
Indwe
Cala Pass
Ku-Mayima
Garryowen
Cala
Luchaba Nature Reserve
White Kei River
Braunville
Askeaton
Whitmore
Lufuta
Satansnek
Ntibane
Cacadu (Lady Frere)
All Saints Nek
Langdon
Nduli Nature Reserve
Qoqodala
Ncora Dam
Engcobo
Coghlan
Bailey
Xonxa Dam
Southeyville
Tsazo
Viedgesville
Bongolo Dam
Lubisi Dam
Bowker's Park
Driver's Drift
Ncora
Clarkebury
Queenstown
Ezibeleni
Isomo River
Nobokwe
Bityi
Mqanduli
Sunken Gardens
Ngqungqu
Bolotwa
Qamata
Garner's Drift
Bashee Bridge
Kamastone
St Marks
Cofimvada
Qombolo
Munyu
Eliotdale
Hange
Tsomo
Colleywobbles
Hukuwa
Tylden
Xolobe
Ntseshe
Idutywa
Alder
Sada
Whittlesea
Guildford
Waqu
Swart Kei River
Bacela
Mbashe River
Ebende
Nqamaqwe
Waterdown Dam
Cathcart
Taleni
Dwesa Nature Reserve
Ciko
Fairford
Katberg Mountains
Bellgrove
Bolo Reserve
Butterworth
Willowvale
Devils Bellows Nek
Nyokana
Nico Malan Pass
Katberg Pass
Toise River
Mgwali
New Nek
Nqabara
Balfour
Katberg
Kologha Forest Reserve
Cats Pass
Qoboqobo
Manubi
Qora Mouth
Seymour
Dohne
Kei Cuttings
Great Kei River Bridge
Mazeppa Bay
Liddleton
Tsolwana Game Reserve
Stutterheim
Kentani
Hogsback
Bethel
Grays
Komga
Tidbury's Toll
Amherst
Upper Tyume
Ross
Prospect
Great Kei River
Wavecrest
Pleasant View
Keiskammahoek
Gaika's Grave
Amabele
Blinkwater
Fort Hare
Mpetu
Qolora Mouth
Fort Beaufort
Martello Tower
Kei Road
Mpongo Park
Quko
Kei Mouth
Rooikrans Dam
Kwelera River
Morgan's Bay
Alice
Middeldrift
Braunschweig
Tainton
Haga-Haga
Macleantown
Gonubie River
Cape Henderson Nature Reserve
King William's Town
Bisho
Nahoon River
Cintsa
Kwa-Pita
Berlin
Breidbach
Fort Willshire
Zwelitsha
Laing Dam
Potsdam
Beacon Bay
Mdantsane
Dawn
Gonubie Mouth
Bonza Bay
Lekfontein
Keiskama River
Sittingbourne
Fort Murray
EAST LONDON
Nahoon
Fort Brown
Breakfast Vlei
Punzana
Fort Glamorgan
Tyata
Chalumna
Committees
Ecca Pass
Kid's Beach
27°E
28°E
31°S
32°S
N6
N2
A2
A4
R726
R393
R392
R58
R344
R396
R56
R61
R67
R351
R352
R345
R346
R400
R63
R349
R347
R72
24
25
31
37

E
F
G
H
33
30°E
31°E
1
2
3
4
5
6
Eastern Cape
KwaZulu/Natal
Sunshine Coast
Hibiscus Coast
Wild Coast
Isipingo
Adams Mission
Kingsburgh
Umgababa
Umkomaas
Clansthal
Scottburgh
Park Rynie
Kelso
Pennington
Sezela
Ifafa Beach
Mtwalume
Turton
Hibberdene
Umzumbe
Southport
Sea Park
Umtentweni
Port Shepstone
Shelley Beach
Uvongo
Margate
Ramsgate
Southbroom
Trafalgar
Trafalgar Point
Palm Beach
Glenmore Beach
Munster
Banner Rest
Port Edward
Riverside
Ixopo
Swartberg
New Amalfi
Sneezewood
Franklin
Cedarville
Umzimkulu Bridge
Umzimkulu
Highflats
Umtwalume Falls
Vernon Crookes Nature Reserve
Umzinto
Braemar
Mkomazi River
Lovu River
Umpambinyoni River
Umtwalume River
Ntatabomvu
822
Mount Currie Nature Reserve
Bisi
Bonny Ridge
Kokstad
Stafford's Post
Bontrand
St Faith's
Colonanek
Ntsizwa
Weza
Harding
Dweshula
Umzumbe River
Brooks Nek
Umtamvuna River
Oribi Gorge Nature Reserve
Fort Donald
Nqabeni
Marburg
Rode
Maxesibani (Mount Ayliff)
Magusheni
Izingolweni
Paddock
Izotsha
Kwabach (Mount Frere)
Ngabeni
Bizana
Redoubt
Trafalgar Marine Reserve
Tabankulu
Umtamvuna Nature Reserve
Tina Bridge
Mzimvubu River
Mzimhlava River
Siphaqeni (Flagstaff)
Impisi
Qumbu
Holy Cross
Umtentu River
Umtentu
Palmerton
Mkambati Nature Reserve
Mkambati
South Sand Bluff
Msikaba River
Lusikisiki
Port Grosvenor
Rock of Execution
Mlengana Pass
Libode
Embotyi
Umzimvubu River
Gemvale
Ntshilini
Port St Johns
Ngqeleni
Old Bunting
Tombo
Silaka Nature Reserve
Notintsila
Hluleka Nature Reserve
Old Morley
Tshani
Coffee Bay
Mnewasa Point
Cwebe Nature Reserve
R617
R612
R56
R61
N2

A
B
C
D
1
2
3
4
5
6
CAPE TOWN
Atlantic Ocean
False Bay
Western Cape
Stellenbosch
Paarl
Wellington
Worcester
Robertson
Montagu
Swellendam
Caledon
Hermanus
Bredasdorp
Somerset West
Strand
Gordon's Bay
Durbanville
Kraaifontein
Milnerton
Parow
Simon's Town
Fish Hoek
Muizenberg
Hout Bay
Malmesbury
Ceres
Tulbagh
Darling
Moorreesburg
Franschhoek
Villiersdorp
Greyton
Riviersonderend
Napier
Struisbaai
L'Agulhas
Cape Agulhas
Cape Point
Cape of Good Hope
Table Mountain 1073
Robben Island
Dassen Island
Hexrivierberge
Kwadousberg
Waboomsberge
Bredasdorpberge
Witteberge
Nouga Hills
34°S
35°S
36°S
20°E
21°E

E
F
G
H
1
2
3
4
5
6
Laingsburg
Vleifontein
Baviaan
Floriskraal Dam
Rooinek
21°E
Dwyka River
Gamka River
Gamkapoort Dam
Bosluiskloof
Prince Albert
Oukloof Dam
22°E
Swartberg Pass
Groot Swartberge
N12
R407
Klaarstroom
Meiringspoort
Vleiland
Seweweeksporat
Seweweeksporat
Rouxpos
R323
Prins River
Prinsrivier Dam
Anysberg
Ladismith
Zoar
Huisrivier Pass
Calitzdorp
Oosgam
R62
Matjiesrivier
Kraaldorings
Kruisrivier
R328
Cango Caves
Grootkraal
Schoemanspoort
Schoemanshoek
De Rust
Olifants River
R341
Dysselsdorp
Oudtshoorn
De Hoop
Plathuis
Brak River
Groot River
Rooiberg Pass
Volmoed
Kamanassie Dam
Kammanassieberge
Koutjie
Buffelsdrif
Daskop
Speelmans Kraal
Warmwaterberg
Warmwaterberg
1352
Lemoenshoek
Brandrivier
Van Wyksdorp
Groot River
R328
N12
N9
Molenrivier
Noll
Outenikuaberge
Robinson Pass
Herold
Montagu Pass
Outeniqua Pass
Kleinplaat
Bergplaas
Karatara
Barrydale
Tradouw
1364
Tradouw Pass
R324
Garcias Pass
Langeberg
Langberg
R327
Cloetes Pass
Ruitersbos
Blanco
George
Wilderness
Wilderness National Park
Barrington
Phantom Pass
Suurbraak
Heidelberg
Riversdale
N2
Herbertsdale
Sinksabrug
Groot Brakrivier
Pacaltsdorp
Rondevlei
Sedgefield
Goukamma Nature Reserve
Buffalo Bay
Walker Point
Brandwag
Du Plessis Pass
Glentana
Herolds Bay
Hartenbos
Askraal
Albertinia
Mossel Bay
Danabaai
Vis Bay
R324
Slang River
R322
Droëvlakte
Gourits River
Johnson's Post
Vleesbaai
Vermaaklikheid
Riethuiskraal
Still Bay-East
R325
Cape Vacca (Kanon Point)
Witsand
Port Beaufort
Gouritsmond
Groot Jongensfontein
Still Bay-West
Infanta-on-River
Cape Barracouta
Cape Infanta
St Sebastian Bay
Indian Ocean
36

A
B
C
D
1
2
3
4
5
6
23°E
24°E
25°E
34°S
35°S
36°S
Perdepoort
Willowmore
Grootrivierhoogte
Groot River
Mount Stewart
Baroe
Greystone
Darlington Dam
Wolwefontein
Kleinpoort
Steytlerville
Buyspoort
Ghwarriepoort
Olifants River
Baviaanskloofberge
Eastern C
Nuwekluf
Zaaimansdal
Kammanassieberge
Western Cape
Kougaberge
Studtis
Sandvlakte
Colekeplaas
Cockscomb
1759
Grootwinterhoekb
Potjiesberg Pass
Uniondale
Buffelsdrif
Uniondale Poort
Speelmans Kraal
Avontuur
Haarlem
Misgund
Smitskraal
Cambria
Melkhoutboom
Swartkops River
Tip Tree
Demistkraal
Patensie
Molenrivier
Noll
1715
Kouga River
Kouga Dam
Andrieskraal
Gamtoos River
Hankey
De Vlug
Louterwater
Joubertina
Prince Alfred Pass
Tsitsikamaberge
Keurbooms River
Kammiebos
Loerie
Homtini Pass
Barrington
Tsitsikamma Coastal National Park
Bloukrans Pass
Grootrivier Pass
Phantom Pass
Paul Sauer Bridge
Kareedouw
Assegaaibos
Van Stadens Wild Flower Reserve
Knysna National Lake Area
Wittedrift
Nature's Valley
Storms River
Clarckson
Kruisfontein
Sedgefield
Buffalo Bay
Knysna
Keurbooms Nature Reserve
Woodlands
Goukamma NR
Walker Point
Brenton-on-Sea
The Heads
Noetzie
Plettenberg Bay
Robberg Nature Reserve
Cape Seal
Humansdorp
Jeffrey's Bay
Aston Bay
St Fr
Paradysstrand
St Francis Bay
Tsitsikamma Point
Oyster Bay
Slangrivier
Cape St Francis
R407
R341
R339
N9
R332
R62
R340
N2
R337
R338
R329
R75
R331
R330

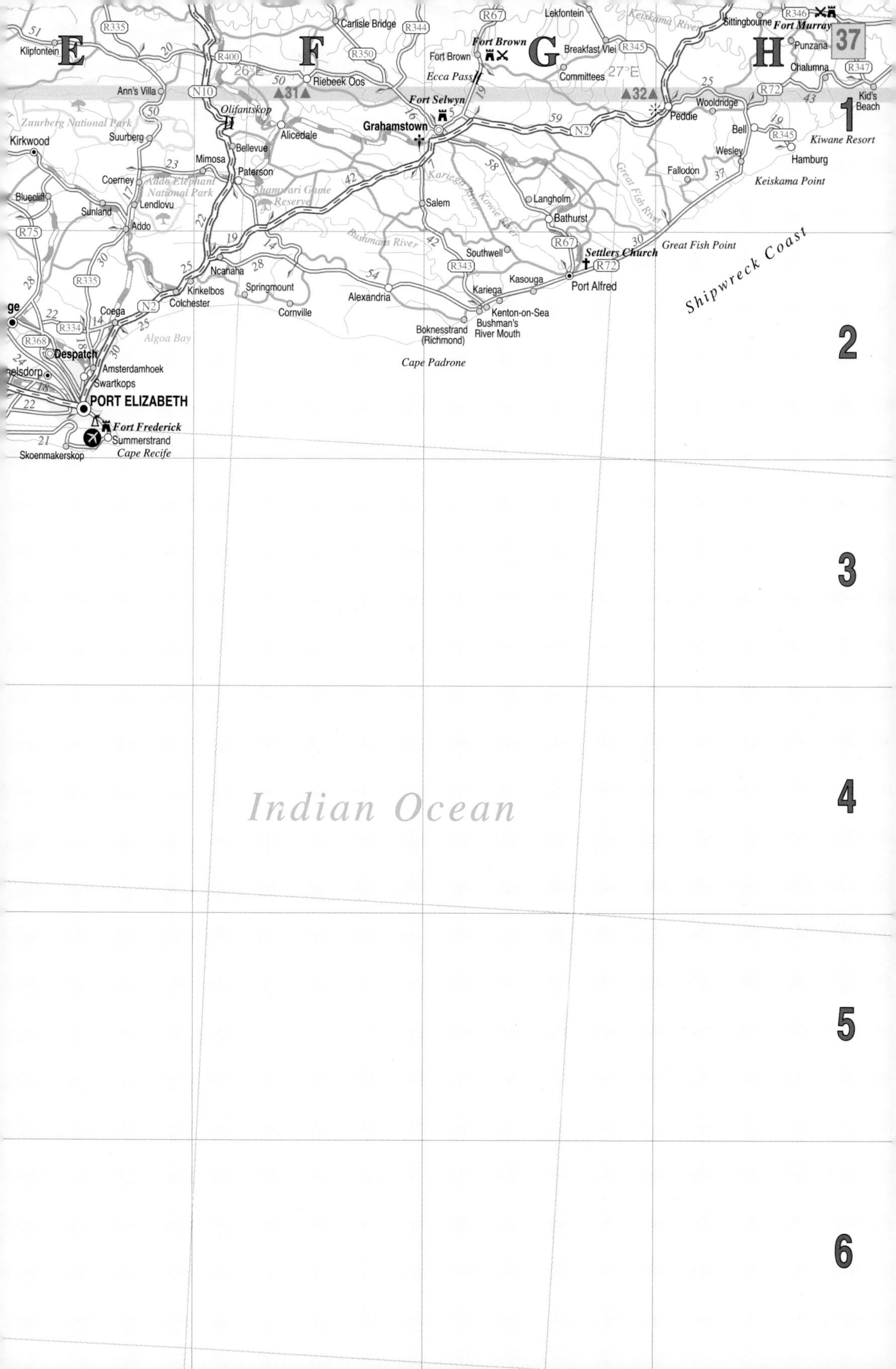
E
F
G
H
1
2
3
4
5
6
Klipfontein
Carlisle Bridge
Lekfontein
Sittingbourne
Fort Murray
Fort Brown
Breakfast Vlei
Punzana
Chalumna
Riebeek Oos
Ecca Pass
Committees
27°E
Ann's Villa
Kid's Beach
Fort Selwyn
Peddie
Wooldridge
Olifantskop
Zuurberg National Park
Suurberg
Grahamstown
Alicedale
Bell
Kiwane Resort
Kirkwood
Bellevue
Wesley
Hamburg
Mimosa
Fallodon
Coerney
Addo Elephant National Park
Paterson
Shamwari Game Reserve
Keiskama Point
Bluecliff
Sunland
Lendlovu
Salem
Langholm
Addo
Bathurst
Kariega River
Kowie River
Great Fish River
Keiskama River
Bushmans River
Southwell
Settlers Church
Great Fish Point
Shipwreck Coast
Ncanaha
Kinkelbos
Springmount
Alexandria
Kariega
Kasouga
Port Alfred
Colchester
Cornville
Kenton-on-Sea
Coega
Boknesstrand (Richmond)
Bushman's River Mouth
Algoa Bay
Despatch
Amsterdamhoek
Cape Padrone
Swartkops
PORT ELIZABETH
Fort Frederick
Summerstrand
Skoenmakerskop
Cape Recife
Indian Ocean
R335
R344
R67
R346
R350
R345
R400
R347
N10
R72
N2
R75
R343
R334
R368
▲31▲
▲32▲

Getting Around South Africa, Lesotho & Swaziland

Bus

In South Africa, Translux runs express services on all the main routes. Tickets must be booked 24 hours in advance. Computicket takes bookings, as do many travel agents and some railway stations. There are also reservations offices around the country.

Transtate's slow buses are cheap and run interesting routes, mainly in the eastern half of the country, with the exception of KwaZulu/Natal. You can't book but that's rarely a problem. Johannesburg is the best place to get information about Transtate, either from their head office or the Jo'burg railway station.

Other major bus lines, such as Greyhound, offer services on much the same routes as Translux, at prices that are usually a little higher. Intercape Mainliner is a major line in the western half of the country and generally charges less than Translux.

There is a good network of slow buses running to many towns in both Lesotho & Swaziland. Minibus taxis are quicker but tend not to run long distances. Prices are similar to those of the Transtate buses in South Africa – which are a little lower than minibus taxi fares. In the more remote areas of Lesotho you might have to arrange a ride with a truck, for which you'll need to negotiate a fare.

Train

In South Africa, trains are comfortable and safe, and fares haven't risen for years. On overnight trains the fare includes a sleeping berth (more expensive private compartments can also be hired) but there's a small charge for bedding hire.

First and 2nd class must be booked 24 hours in advance; you can't book 3rd class. Destinations from Johannesburg include Port Elizabeth, Cape Town and Durban.

Some people come to South Africa just to ride the famous *Blue Train*, running between Pretoria/Johannesburg and Cape Town. This 25-hour journey is one of the world's most luxurious train trips. If you can't afford to take the whole trip, consider a section. *Blue Train* bookings can be made in Johannesburg and through many railway stations and travel agents.

There are no passenger services in Lesotho or Swaziland.

Minibus Taxi

For ultra-long-distance trips in South Africa, minibus taxis can be uncomfortable and also risky because of tired (or drunk) drivers, but for hops between neighbouring towns they are a good way to get around.

In tiny Lesotho and Swaziland ultra-long-distances are not possible, so minibus taxis are the obvious mode of public transport. Minibuses can't cope with some of Lesotho's rough roads and can be very uncomfortable if they try. Choose a bus for a long trip.

Car & Motorcycle

Most major roads in South Africa are excellent and carry little traffic, and off the big roads are

RICHARD EVERIST

Cape Gannet rookery, Lambert's Bay, Western Cape Province

some interesting backroads to explore. The country is crossed by National Routes (N1 etc), and some sections of these are toll roads. Tolls can vary widely. There is always an alternative route.

Driving in Lesotho is getting easier as new roads are built in conjunction with the Highlands Water Project, but once you get off the tar there are still plenty of places where even a 4WD vehicle will get into trouble. Apart from rough roads, rivers flooding after summer storms present the biggest problems, and you can be stuck for days. People and animals on the roads are another hazard.

Most main roads in Swaziland are quite good as long as you don't speed, and there are also some satisfyingly rough backroads through the bush. The main dangers are again people and animals on the road. If an official motorcade approaches, you must pull over and stop.

Road Rules You can use your usual driving licence if it carries your photo, otherwise you'll need an International Driving Permit. Wearing seat belts is compulsory in all three countries, and in all you must drive on the left.

The speed limit in South Africa is 100 km/h (roughly 60 miles per hour), 120 km/h on most highways. The usual limit in towns is 60 km/h. In Swaziland and Lesotho the highway limit is 80 km/h.

There are a few local variations on road rules. The main one is the 'four-way stop'. If there are other vehicles at this type of intersection, those which arrived first have right of way.

Rental The major international companies, such as Avis and Budget, have offices or agents across South Africa. Their rates are high, but if you book through your local agent at home before you arrive they will be significantly lower.

JON MURRAY

Sculpture at Victoria and Alfred Waterfront, Cape Town, West Province

The larger local South African companies include Imperial, Tempest and Dolphin. A step down from these are smaller and cheaper outfits such as Alisa and Panther which can be found in Johannesburg and Cape Town.

Car rental is available in Swaziland and, at very high rates, in Lesotho. You usually can take a car hired in South Africa into Lesotho or Swaziland, but you might need to get a special letter of authorisation from your rental company.

Camper Vans A way around high accommodation and transport costs is to hire a camper van. One company with a range of deals is Leisure Mobiles in Johannesburg.

Bicycle

South Africa is a good country to cycle in, with a wide variety of terrain and climate, plenty of camping places and many good roads, most of which don't carry a lot of traffic. Most of the National Routes are too busy for comfort, although there are quieter sections, especially in northern KwaZulu/Natal and the Cape provinces.

Being small and friendly, Swaziland would be a good country to explore by bike. The main road between Mbabane and Manzini is too narrow and busy for safe riding. Serious mountain bikers could have some wild times in Lesotho.

Comment Circuler en Afrique du Sud, au Lesotho et au Ngwane

Bus

En Afrique du Sud, Translux assure un service express sur les principaux itinéraires. Les places se réservent au moins 24h à l'avance, soit auprès de Computicket, soit dans les agences de voyages. Certaines gares délivrent également des billets et il existe des bureaux de réservations un peu partout dans le pays.

Les bus Transtate, plus lents mais aussi moins chers, suivent des itinéraires souvent intéressants, surtout dans la moitié est du pays. C'est à Johannesburg que l'on vous renseignera le mieux sur cette compagnie, soit au bureau central de la compagnie, soit à la gare de Jo'burg.

Parmi les autres grandes compagnies routières de passagers, Greyhound dessert les mêmes destinations que Translux à des prix légèrement supérieurs. En revanche, Inter-cape Mainliner, surtout présent dans l'ouest du pays, coûte généralement moins cher que Translux.

Il existe un bon réseau de bus au Lesotho et au Ngwane, mais ce sont des véhicules assez lents. Si les taxis-minibus peuvent faire gagner du temps, rares sont ceux qui acceptent de parcourir de longues distances. Les tarifs des bus sont similaires à ceux de Transtate, en Afrique du Sud, c'est-à-dire légèrement inférieurs aux prix des taxis-minibus. Dans certaines zones reculées du Lesotho, il n'existe pas de transports en commun. Il faut donc avoir recours à des camions : à vous, dans ce cas, de négocier le prix avec le chauffeur.

Train

Les trains sud-africains sont sûrs et confortables. Leurs tarifs n'ont pas augmenté depuis des années. Dans les trains de nuit, le prix du billet comprend la couchette (un voyage en wagon-lit, également possible, revient plus cher), mais il faut prévoir un petit supplément pour la location de draps et de couvertures.

Première et seconde classes se réservent impérativement au moins 24h à l'avance. Les billets de troisième, pour leur part, s'achètent au dernier moment. Parmi les destinations desservies au départ de Johannesburg, figurent Port Elizabeth, Le Cap et Durban.

Certaines personnes viennent surtout en Afrique du Sud pour embarquer à bord du célèbre *Blue Train* qui relie Pretoria/Johannesburg au Cap. Ce trajet de 25 heures compte parmi les voyages ferroviaires les plus luxueux du monde. Si vous ne pouvez vous l'offrir en entier, envisagez de ne parcourir qu'une partie du trajet. Les réservations pour le *Blue Train* se font à Johannesburg, ainsi que dans les gares de plusieurs autres villes et auprès des agences de voyages.

Au Lesotho et au Ngwane, aucun train ne prend de voyageurs.

Taxi-Minibus

Il est déconseillé d'entreprendre un très long trajet en taxi-minibus en Afrique du Sud. Le voyage devient en effet vite inconfortable et les risques liés à la fatigue du chauffeur (ou à son taux d'alcoolémie !) sont loin d'être négligeables. En revanche, ce mode de transport est idéal pour les déplacements d'une ville à une autre.

La situation diffère au Lesotho et au Ngwane, petits pays où les distances sont courtes. Là, le taxi-minibus représente le mode de locomotion idéal. Toutefois, sachez que ces véhicules peinent sur les mauvaises routes : le voyage devient alors très inconfortable pour les passagers. Pour un long trajet, préférez donc le bus.

Voiture et Moto

La plupart des grandes routes d'Afrique du Sud sont excellentes et peu fréquentées. En dehors des principaux itinéraires, il existe également de

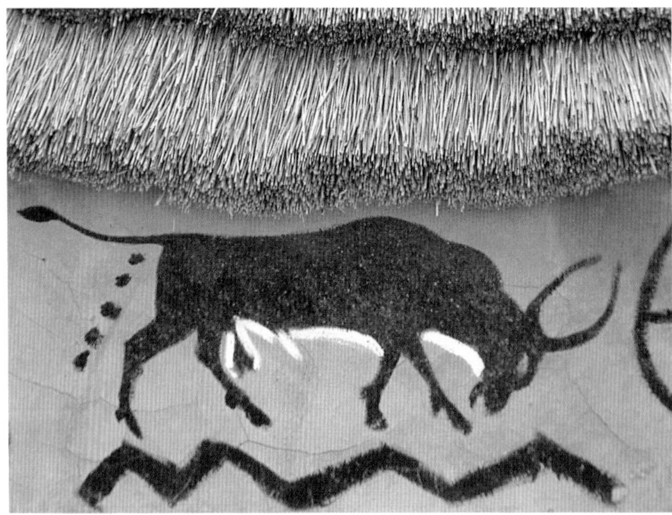

RICHARD EVERIST

Hand-painted motifs adorn buildings in Lotlamoreng Cultural Village, near Mmabatho, North-West Province

petites routes très intéressantes à explorer. Le pays est sillonné par des routes nationales (N1, etc.), dont certaines sections sont payantes. Les prix varient beaucoup d'un péage à un autre, mais il existe toujours un itinéraire parallèle.

La conduite devient plus facile qu'auparavant au Lesotho, où la construction de nouvelles routes se poursuit dans le cadre du Highlands Water Project (projet d'irrigation des régions montagneuses). Dès que l'on quitte le bitume, toutefois, il reste d'innombrables secteurs où même un véhicule 4x4 peut rencontrer de sérieuses difficultés. Outre le mauvais état des routes, les crues des rivières liées aux violents orages de l'été posent de lourds problèmes, et l'on peut se retrouver bloqué quelque part pendant plusieurs jours. Enfin, méfiez-vous des piétons et des animaux qui marchent sur les routes. Si vous voyez arriver un cortège de voitures officielles, vous devez impérativement vous arrêter pour le laisser passer.

Code de la route S'il comporte une photographie, votre permis de conduire habituel suffit. Dans le cas contraire, vous devrez vous procurer un permis international (International Driving Permit) auprès de votre préfecture. Le port de la ceinture de sécurité est obligatoire dans les trois pays, où l'on conduit à gauche.

En Afrique du Sud, la vitesse est limitée à 100 km/h sur les routes, 120 km/h sur la plupart des autoroutes et 60 km/h en ville. Au Lesotho et au Ngwane, la limite est fixée à 80 km/h sur autoroute.

Il existe par ailleurs quelques variantes locales au code de la route traditionnel. La principale concerne les carrefours : le véhicule qui s'engage le premier a la priorité.

Voitures de location Les loueurs les plus connus dans le monde, comme Avis et Hertz, possèdent des bureaux ou de simples guichets dans toute l'Afrique du Sud. Leurs tarifs sont élevés et vous ferez de sérieuses économies en réservant le véhicule avant le départ, dans votre pays d'origine.

Parmi les grandes compagnies locales, citons Imperial, Tempest et Dolphin. Alisa et Panther, plus modestes et moins chères, sont présentes à Johannesburg et au Cap.

On peut aussi louer une voiture au Ngwane et, à des prix nettement supérieurs, au Lesotho. En général, il est possible de se rendre dans ces deux pays au volant d'une voiture louée en Afrique du Sud, mais il peut arriver que l'on vous réclame une lettre d'autorisation spéciale délivrée par le loueur.

Camping-cars Pour pallier aux prix élevés de l'hébergement et des transports, le camping-car représente une bonne solution. Leisure Mobiles, à Johannesburg, propose plusieurs solutions de location.

Bicyclette

Avec sa végétation et son climat variés, ses nombreux terrains de camping et ses bonnes routes, peu fréquentées pour la plupart, l'Afrique du Sud se prête bien aux déplacements en bicyclette. Certes, les routes nationales sont trop passantes pour permettre aux cyclistes de rouler en toute tranquillité, mais il en existe néanmoins certaines sections plus calmes, surtout au nord, dans les provinces du KwaZulu/Natal et du Cap.

Au Ngwane, pays sympathique et peu étendu, les cyclotouristes devraient pouvoir s'en donner à cœur joie, à condition d'éviter la route reliant Mbabane à Manzini, étroite et très fréquentée. En revanche, le relief accidenté du Lesotho risque de donner du fil à retordre aux cyclistes les plus chevronnés.

JON MURRAY

The Namastat's beehive huts, Springbok, Northern Cape Province

Reisen in Südafrika, Lesotho und Swasiland

Bus

Translux setzt in Südafrika Expressdienste auf allen Hauptstrecken ein. Fahrkarten müssen 24 Stunden im voraus gebucht werden. Computicket, wie auch viele Reisebüros und einige Bahnhöfe führen Buchungen durch. Daneben gibt es noch überall im Land Reservierungsbüros.

Die langsamen Transtate Busse sind billig und verkehren auf interessanten Strecken, vor allem in der Osthälfte des Landes mit Ausnahme von KwaZulu/Natal. Man kann nicht im voraus buchen, aber das ist selten ein Problem. In Johannesburg kann man sich am besten über Transtate Dienste informieren, und zwar entweder bei der Transtate Hauptgeschäftsstelle oder im Hauptbahnhof Johannesburg.

Andere große Busunternehmen, wie Greyhound, verkehren auf etwa den gleichen Strecken wie Translux zu normalerweise etwas höheren Preisen. Intercape Mainliner ist eine große Linie in der Westhälfte des Landes und ist im allgemeinen etwas billiger als Translux.

In Lesotho und Swasiland verbindet ein gutes Netz langsamer Busse viele Städte.

Minibustaxis sind schneller aber fahren meist keine Langstrecken. Die Preise sind vergleichbar mit den Transtate Busen in Südafrika – ein bißchen günstiger als die Tarife der Minibustaxis. In den etwas abgelegeneren Ecken Lesothos muß man eventuell eine Fahrt mit einem LKW arrangieren. Hierbei ist der Fahrpreis Verhandlungssache.

Zug

Südafrikas Züge sind komfortabel und sicher. Und die Fahrpreise sind seit Jahren nicht gestiegen. Bei Nachtzügen ist ein Bett im Fahrpreis inbegriffen (man kann auch etwas teurere Einzelabteile buchen) während für das Ausleihen von Bettzeug eine kleine Gebühr erhoben wird.

Fahrkarten für die erste und zweite Klasse müssen 24 Stunden im voraus gebucht werden. Fahrkarten dritter Klasse lassen sich nicht vorbestellen. Reiseziele ab Johannesburg schließen Port Elizabeth, Kapstadt und Durban ein.

RICHARD EVERIST

The crane flower

Es gibt Leute, die nur nach Südafrika kommen, um mit dem berühmten *Blue Train* zu fahren, der zwischen Pretoria/Johannesburg und Kapstadt verkehrt. Diese 25-stündige Reise gehört zu den prächtigsten Zugfahrten der Welt. Wenn man sich nicht die ganze Fahrt leisten kann, sollte man wenigstens einen Teilabschnitt in Erwägung ziehen. Buchungen für den *Blue Train* kann man in Johannesburg und durch viele Bahnhöfe und Reisebüros vornehmen lassen.

In Lesotho und Swasiland gibt es keinen Passagierverkehr.

Minibustaxi

Die Minibustaxis in Südafrika können bei extrem langen Fahrten unbequem und wegen der übermüdeten (oder betrunkenen) Fahrer risikoreich sein. Für Kurzstrecken zwischen benachbarten Städten jedoch sind sie ein gutes Reisemittel.

Im kleinen Lesotho und Swasiland sind extrem lange Strecken gar nicht möglich. Daher liegt es nahe, Minibustaxis als Verkehrsmittel zu benutzen. Minibusse sind für einige der holprigen Straßen nicht geeignet und können daher äußerst unbequem sein. Für eine lange Reise empfiehlt sich ein Bus.

Auto & Motorrad

Die meisten Hauptstraßen in Südafrika sind hervorragend und führen wenig Verkehr. Und abseits der großen Straßen gibt es viele interessante Nebenstraßen zu erkunden. Das Land ist von Nationalstraßen durchzogen (N1 etc.) und davon sind einige Abschnitte gebührenpflichtig. Die Gebühren können sehr unterschiedlich sein. Und es gibt immer eine Alternativstrecke.

In Lesotho wird das Fahren einfacher, da neue Straßen in

Verbindung mit dem Hochland Wasserprojekt gebaut werden. Aber abseits von den geteerten Straßen gibt es immer noch viele Stellen, an denen sogar ein Geländefahrzeug seine Probleme hat. Neben unebenen Straßen stellen angeschwollene Flüsse nach Hitzegewittern das größte Problem dar. Es kann passieren, daß man tagelang festsitzt. Eine zusätzliche Gefahr sind Menschen und Tiere auf der Fahrbahn.

In Swasiland sind die meisten Hauptstraßen ziemlich gut, solange man langsam fährt. Daneben gibt es noch ein paar ausreichend holprige Nebenstraßen durch den Busch. Wieder stellen Menschen und Tiere die Hauptgefahr auf den Straßen dar. Wenn sich eine offizielle Autokolonne nähert, muß man an die Seite fahren und anhalten.

Verkehrsregeln Man kann den nationalen Führerschein benutzen, solange dieser ein Foto enthält. Andernfalls benötigt man einen internationalen Führerschein. Es besteht in allen drei Ländern Anschnallpflicht und es herrscht Linksverkehr.

Die Geschwindigkeitsbegrenzung in Südafrika liegt bei 100 km/h (etwa 60 Meilen pro Stunde) und 120 km/h auf den meisten Fernstraßen. In Ortschaften gilt normalerweise 60 km/h. In Swasiland und Lesotho ist die Höchstgeschwindigkeit auf Fernstraßen 80 km/h.

Es gibt nur wenige ortsübliche Abweichungen von den allgemeinen Verkehrsregeln. Die Hauptausnahme ist der "Vier-Wege-Stop". Bei diesem Kreuzungstyp hat derjenige Vorfahrt, der zuerst ankommt.

Autovermietung Die internationalen großen Firmen wie Avis und Budget haben Niederlassungen oder Vertretungen in ganz Südafrika. Die Kosten sind

JON MURRAY

Minaret on a Durban Mosque

hoch. Wenn man jedoch schon vor der Reise durch das örtliche Reisebüro von Zuhause bucht, wird es wesentlich günstiger.

Zu den größeren lokalen südafrikanischen Unternehmen gehören Imperial, Tempest und Dolphin. Eine Stufe darunter kommen die kleineren und billigeren Läden wie Alisa und Panther in Johannesburg und Kapstadt.

Es gibt Autovermietungen in Swasiland, und zu sehr hohen Preisen auch in Lesotho. Normalerweise darf man einen Mietwagen aus Südafrika mit nach Lesotho oder Swasiland nehmen. Eventuell benötigt man jedoch ein spezielles Genehmigungsschreiben vom Autovermieter.

Wohnmobil Eine Möglichkeit, hohe Übernachtungs- und Transportkosten zu vermeiden, ist ein Wohnmobil zu mieten. Leisure Mobiles in Johannesburg ist ein Unternehmen mit einer Reihe von Angeboten.

Fahrrad

Südafrika eignet sich gut zum Fahrradfahren mit seiner großen Gelände- und Klimavielfalt, vielen Campingplätzen und vielen guten Straßen, wovon die meisten wenig befahren sind. Die meisten Nationalstraßen sind zu stark befahren um angenehm zu sein. Es gibt allerdings ruhigere Strecken, besonders im nördlichen KwaZulu/Natal und in den Kapbezirken.

Als kleines und freundliches Land wäre Swasiland eigentlich ein Land, welches sich zum Entdecken per Fahrrad anbieten würde. Die Hauptstraße zwischen Mbabane und Manzini ist zu schmal und verkehrsreich für sicheres Fahrradfahren. Ernsthafte Mountainbike Fahrer könnten in Lesotho eine wilde Zeit haben.

Cómo Movilizarse en África del Sur, Lesotho y Suazilandia

En Autobús

En África del Sur, la compañía Translux ofrece servicios expresos en todas las rutas principales. Los boletos deben comprarse con 24 horas de anticipación. Pueden hacerse las reservas en Computiket y en muchas agencias de viajes así como también en algunas estaciones de ferrocarril. Además, hay oficinas para reservas en todo el país.

Los lentos autobuses de Transtate son baratos y recorren rutas interesantes, principalmente en la zona este del país, con la excepción de Kwazulú/Natal. Pueden hacerse reservas, aunque esto no es un problema. El mejor lugar para encontrar información sobre Transtate es Johannesburgo, bien en la oficina principal o en la estación de ferrocarril.

Otras líneas importantes, como la Greyhound, ofrecen servicios prácticamente en las mismas rutas que la Translux a precios que normalmente son un poco más altos. Intercape Mainliner es una línea importante en la mitad oeste del país y, generalmente, es más barata que Translux.

En Lesotho y Suazilandia existe una buena red de autobuses lentos que van a muchos pueblos. Los taxis minibús son más rápidos, pero generalmente no recorren largas distancias. Los precios son similares a los de los autobuses Transtate de África del Sur – que son un poco más baratos que los pasajes de los taxis minibús. En las zonas más remotas de Lesotho quizás tenga que concertar el viaje con un camionero, para lo que tendrá que negociar el precio.

En Tren

En África del Sur, los trenes son confortables y seguros y los precios no han aumentado por años. En los viajes nocturnos, el precio incluye una cama (pueden alquilarse compartimientos privados pero éstos son más caros) pero hay que pagar un pequeño sobrecargo por el alquiler de la ropa de cama.

La primera y la segunda clases deben reservarse con 24 horas de anticipación; no se pueden hacer reservas para la 3ª clase. Los destinos desde Johannesburgo incluyen Port Elizabeth, El Cabo y Durban.

Algunas personas van a África del Sur tan sólo para viajar en el famoso *Blue Train* (el Tren Azul), que hace el recorrido entre Pretoria/Johannesburgo y El Cabo. Este es un viaje de 25 horas y es uno de los viajes en tren más lujosos del mundo. Si el viaje completo no entra dentro de su presupuesto, considere viajar una sección. Las reservas para el *Blue Train* pueden hacerse en Johannesburgo y en muchas estaciones de ferrocarril y agencias de viaje.

No existen servicios para pasajeros ni en Lesotho ni en Suazilandia.

En Taxi Minibús

Para los viajes muy largos en África del Sur los taxis minibús pueden resultar incómodos y además peligrosos debido al cansancio (o borrachera) de los conductores, pero para movilizarse entre pueblos vecinos son una buena manera de viajar.

En los pequeños Lesotho y Sualizandia no existen las largas distancias, por lo que los taxis minibús son la forma obvia de transporte público. Los minibuses no pueden con el terreno accidentado de algunas de las carreteras de Lesotho y pueden resultar muy incómodos cuando se aventuran a recorrerlos. Para un viaje largo tome el autobús.

DI JONES

Traditional 'Sangoma' or herbalist, Lesotho

Coche y Motocicleta

La mayoría de las carreteras en África del Sur son excelentes y con poco tráfico y desde ellas se puede ir a explorar desviándose a interesantísimas carreteras menos importantes. El país está cruzado por Rutas Nacionales (N1 etc), y en algunas secciones hay que pagar peaje. El peaje varía mucho, pero siempre hay una ruta alternativa.

El manejar por Lesotho está mejorando ya que se están construyendo nuevas carreteras en cooperación con el Proyecto de Aguas de las Tierras Altas, pero una vez se deja el asfalto todavía existen muchos lugares donde incluso un vehículo de tracción a cuatro ruedas tendrá dificultades. Además de las carreteras accidentadas, el problema más serio son las inundaciones producidas por los ríos después de las tormentas del verano. Uno puede quedarse inmovilizado durante días. Otro problema son las personas y los animales que andan por la carretera.

La mayoría de las carreteras en Suazilandia son bastante buenas si no se corre demasiado, y también hay algunas carreteras secundarias accidentadas que atraviesan la campiña que le satisfarán. El mayor peligro, una vez más, son las personas y los animales en la carretera. Si se acercara una caravana oficial de coches, usted debe ponerse a un lado y parar.

Reglas de la Carretera Usted puede usar su licencia normal de conducir si ésta lleva foto, de no ser así usted necesitará una licencia internacional de conducir. En los tres países es obligatorio usar los cinturones de seguridad y en los tres se circula por la izquierda.

En África del Sur la velocidad máxima es de 100 km/h (aproximadamente 60 millas por hora), 120 en la mayoría de las carreteras importantes. Normalmente en los pueblos la velocidad máxima es de 60 km/h. En Suazilandia y Lesotho la velocidad máxima es de 80 km/h.

Existen algunas diferencias locales en las reglas de tráfico. La más importante es 'la parada de cuatro direcciones' (fourway stop). En este tipo de intersección, el que llega antes tiene la preferencia de paso.

Alquiler Las compañías más importantes, como Avis y Budget, tienen oficinas o agentes en toda el África del Sur. Las tarifas son altas, pero resultarán mucho más baratas si hace la reserva a través de su agente de viajes antes de llegar.

Entre las mayores compañías locales están Imperial, Tempest y Dolphin. Con un poco menos de categoría están otras más pequeñas y más baratas como Alisa y Panther ubicadas en Johannesburgo y El Cabo.

Se pueden obtener coches de alquiler en Suazilandia y, a precios muy altos, en Lesotho. Normalmente se pueden llevar a Lesotho y Suazilandia los coches alquilados en África del Sur, pero puede que usted necesite una carta especial de autorización de la compañía de alquiler.

Furgonetas para Acampar (Camper Vans) Una manera de ahorrar dinero en el alto coste del alojamiento y del transporte es alquilar una furgoneta de acampar. La compañía Leisure Movile de Johannesburgo ofrece varias opciones.

En Bicicleta

África del Sur es un buen país para viajar en bicicleta, con gran variedad de terrenos y climas, muchos lugares para acampar y muchas carreteras buenas, de las cuales la mayoría no tienen mucha circulación. La mayoría de las Rutas Nacionales tienen demasiado tráfico para poder disfrutar, aunque hay tramos tranquilos, especialmente en el norte de la provincia de Kwazulú/Natal y en la provincia de El Cabo.

Por ser pequeño y amistoso, Suazilandia es un buen país para explorar en bicicleta. La carretera principal entre Mbabane y Manzini es demasiado estrecha y congestionada para la seguridad en bicicleta. Los ciclistas de montaña experimentados pueden disfrutar mucho en Lesotho.

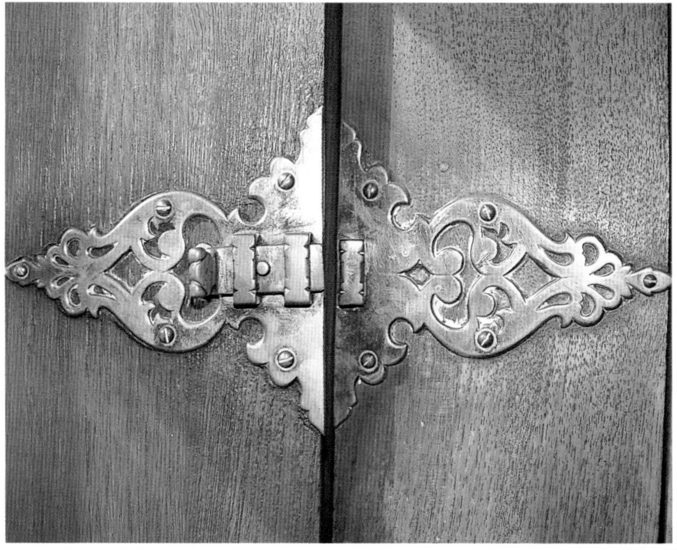

JON MURRAY

Ornate cupboard lock from the days of the VOC

バス

南アフリカのすべての主要ルートはトランスラックス社(Translux)が急行便を運行している。チケットは出発の24時間前に予約する必要がある。旅行代理店、いくつかの鉄道の駅以外にコンピュチケット(Computicket)で予約を受け付けている。国内には予約受付所がたくさんある。

トランステート社(Transtate)のバスは遅いが安く、クワズル(KwaZulu)／ナタル(Natal)を除く東部を主に走るが、これらのルートはけっこう面白い。予約はできないがそのために起こるトラブルはほとんどない。トランステートの情報が最も得やすいのはヨハネスバーグ(Johannesburg)だ。ヨハネスバーグの本社、または鉄道のヨハネスバーグ駅などで入手できる。

RICHARD EVERIST

Impala, Kalahari Gemsbok National Park, Northern Cape Province

このほかに、グレイハウンドなどの主要バス会社もトランスラックスとほぼ同じルートを運行しているが料金は少々高めだ。西部をカバーする主なバス会社はインターケープ・メインライナー社(Intercape Mainliner)で、料金はトランスラックスより安いことが多い。

レソトおよびスワジランドはバスのネットワークが発達し、スピードは遅いがさまざまな町をつないでいる。料金は南アフリカのトランステートなどとほぼ同じだが、これはミニバスタクシーよりやや安い。レソトの田舎に行くにはトラックに便乗させてもらえるよう自分でアレンジしなくてはいけない。料金をあらかじめ交渉しておくこと。

電車

南アフリカの電車は乗り心地が良く安全で、料金は何年も変わっていない。夜行列車の料金には寝台使用料も含まれている(さらに高価な個人用の寝台室も借りることができる)が、シーツなどの寝具のレンタル料は小額だが別に払う。

一等席と二等席は24時間前に予約が必要だが、三等席の予約はできない。ヨハネスバーグからの行き先はポート・エリザベス(Port Elizabeth)、ケープタウン(Cape Town)、ダーバン(Durban)などがある。

旅行者のなかには、プリトリア(Pretoria)－ヨハネスバーグ、ケープタウン間を走る有名なブルー・トレイン*(Blue Train)*に乗るためだけに南アフリカを訪れる人もいる。この25時間の列車の旅は世界で一番豪華なもののひとつだ。全行程の旅が高すぎる場合は、区間の一部だけに乗ることもできるので、それも考慮に入れるといい。ブルー・トレインの予約はヨハネスバーグか鉄道の駅、旅行代理店でできる。

レソトとスワジランドには旅客列車は走っていない。

ミニバス・タクシー

南アフリカの超長距離旅行をする際、ミニバス・タクシーは乗り心地が悪く、運転手が疲れる(または酔払い運転をする)ので危険な場合もある。しかし近隣の町をちょっと旅行する程度ならとても便利だ。

レソトやスワジランドは国土が狭いから超長距離旅行はそもそも不可能なので、ミニバス・タクシーが最も良く使われる公共交通機関だが、レソトのでこぼこ道に対する耐久性がなく走ったとしても大変乗り心地が悪い。長距離旅行にはバスを薦める。

自動車とオートバイ

南アフリカの幹線道路は状態がとても良く交通量も少ない。また、大通りを離れると、面白い裏道路がいくつかある。国道(N１号線など)が国内を貫いており、いくつかの区間は有料で料金はさまざまだ。たいてい有料区間を避けるルートがある。

レソトはハイランド・ウォーター・プロジェクトに関連して新しい道路が建設されているので運転が次第に楽になってきているが、舗装道路を離れると四駆でも危険なところがまだ数多くある。道がでこぼこという以外には、夏のストーム後の川の洪水がもっとも大きな問題で、何日も足止めを食うことがある。路上の人々と動物が原因で起こる事故も問題点の一つだ。

スワジランドのほとんどの幹線道路はスピードの出し過ぎさえしなければ安全だ。また、ブッシュを貫く田舎道もいくつかあり楽しめる。この国でも路上の人と動物がもっとも危険な障害物だ。公務のための自動車の列が向かってきたら端によけて止まらなくてはいけない。

交通規則：運転免許証に写真が貼付されていれば、日常使っているもので大丈夫だが、写真が付いてなければ国際免許証(International Driving Permit) が必要だ。この3国ともすべて、左側通行でシートベルトの着用が義務づけられている。

南アフリカの制限速度は時速100km(約時速 60マイル)、ほとんどのハイウェイでは時速120km。町中の制限速度はふつう60km。スワジランドとレソトのハイウェイの制限速度は時速80km。

地域によっていくつか交通規則が異なが、そのうち、主なものに十字路のルールがある。このような交差点では初めにその地点に着いた車が最優先となる。

レンタカー：南アフリカ国内にはエイヴィス(Avis)やバジェット(Budget)などの国際的な主要レンタカー会社の営業所や支店がいたるところにある。レンタル料は高いが、出発前に自国の営業所であらかじめ予約すると大変安くなる。

現地の主な会社にはインペリアル(Imperial)、テンペスト(Tempest)、ドルフィン(Dolphin)などがある。ランクが一つ下になるが、ヨハネスバーグとケープタウンには小さくて安い車のアリサ(Alisa)、パンサー(Panther)などがある。

スワジランドとレソトにもレンタカーがあるが、レソトでは料金が大変高い。南アフリカで借りたレンタカーをレソトやスワジランドに持ち込むことはふつう可能だが、レンタカー会社からの特別認可状が必要なことがある。

キャンピングカー：高い宿泊料、レンタカー料を避けるにはキャンピングカーを借りるのが良い。キャンピングカーの種類を多く取り揃えている会社には、ヨハネスバーグのレジャー・モービルズ(Leisure Mobiles)などがある。

自転車

南アフリカはサイクリングするには抜群の国だ。地形や天候がバラエティーに富んでる上にキャンプ場がたくさんあり、道路は整っていてそのほとんどが公通量もさほど多くない。国道(National Route)のほとんどは交通量が多く、気楽な旅ができるとはいえないが、その中では特にクワズル／ナタール県の北部やケープ県は交通量が少ない。

スワジランドは小さくフレンドリーなので、自転車でめぐるにはいい国だ。ムババネ(Mbabane)ーマンジニ(Manzini)間は道が狭く混んでいるので安全ではない。レソトはマウンテンバイクを真剣にやりたい人にとってとてもワイルドに楽しめるところだ。

GLENN BEANLAND

Traditional Swazi handicrafts

Index

Note: Geographical and cultural features are also listed separately at the end of the general index in their appropriate categories.

GENERAL INDEX

All places are in South Africa except:

B - Botswana
L - Lesotho
M - Mozambique
N - Namibia
S - Swaziland
Z - Zimbabwe

For duplicate names in South Africa, the province abbreviations are:

EC - Eastern Cape
FS - Free State
G - Gauteng
K - KwaZulu/Natal
Mp - Mpumalanga
NC - Northern Cape
NP - Northern Province
NW - North-West
WC - Western Cape

BORDER GATES

CAMPS AND LODGES

NATIONAL PARKS AND NATURE RESERVES

RIVERS, LAKES, BAYS AND DAMS

RUINS AND MONUMENTS

SPRINGS

VALLEYS

VIEW POINTS

PLANET TALK

Lonely Planet's FREE quarterly newsletter

We love hearing from you and think you'd like to hear from us.

When...is the right time to see reindeer in Finland?
Where...can you hear the best palm-wine music in Ghana?
How...do you get from Asunción to Areguá by steam train?
What...is the best way to see India?

For the answer to these and many other questions read PLANET TALK.

Every issue is packed with up-to-date travel news and advice including:

- a letter from Lonely Planet co-founders Tony and Maureen Wheeler
- go behind the scenes on the road with a Lonely Planet author
- feature article on an important and topical travel issue
- a selection of recent letters from travellers
- details on forthcoming Lonely Planet promotions
- complete list of Lonely Planet products

lonely planet
FREE QUARTERLY NEWSLETTER
PLANET TALK
JANUARY–MARCH 1997
Florida's Spirit Guides & Battlegrounds

To join our mailing list contact any Lonely Planet office.

Also available: Lonely Planet T-shirts. 100% heavyweight cotton.

LONELY PLANET ONLINE

Get the latest travel information before you leave or while you're on the road

Whether you've just begun planning your next trip, or you're chasing down specific info on currency regulations or visa requirements, check out the Lonely Planet World Wide Web site for up-to-the-minute travel information.

As well as travel profiles of your favourite destinations (including interactive maps and full-colour photos), you'll find current reports from our army of researchers and other travellers, updates on health and visas, travel advisories, and the ecological and political issues you need to be aware of as you travel.

There's an online travellers' forum (the Thorn Tree) where you can share your experiences of life on the road, meet travel companions and ask other travellers for their recommendations and advice. We also have plenty of links to other Web sites useful to independent travellers.

With tens of thousands of visitors a month, the Lonely Planet Web site is one of the most popular on the Internet and has won a number of awards including GNN's Best of the Net travel award.

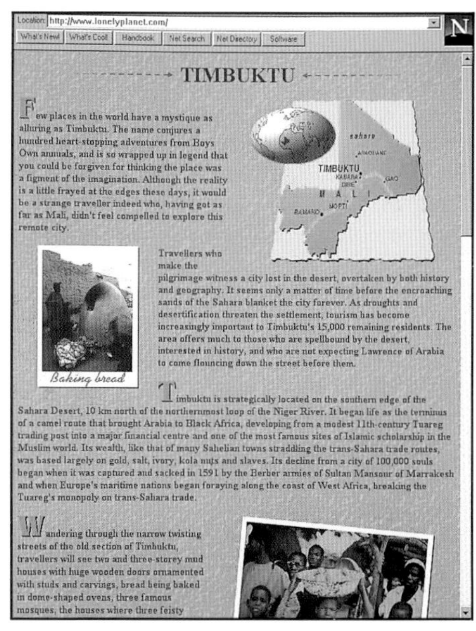
Location: http://www.lonelyplanet.com/
What's New! | What's Cool! | Handbook | Net Search | Net Directory | Software

TIMBUKTU

Few places in the world have a mystique as alluring as Timbuktu. The name conjures a hundred heart-stopping adventures from Boys Own annuals, and is so wrapped up in legend that you could be forgiven for thinking the place was a figment of the imagination. Although the reality is a little frayed at the edges these days, it would be a strange traveller indeed who, having got as far as Mali, didn't feel compelled to explore this remote city.

Baking bread

Travellers who make the pilgrimage witness a city lost in the desert, overtaken by both history and geography. It seems only a matter of time before the encroaching sands of the Sahara blanket the city forever. As droughts and desertification threaten the settlement, tourism has become increasingly important to Timbuktu's 15,000 remaining residents. The area offers much to those who are spellbound by the desert, interested in history, and who are not expecting Lawrence of Arabia to come flouncing down the street before them.

Timbuktu is strategically located on the southern edge of the Sahara Desert, 10 km north of the northernmost loop of the Niger River. It began life as the terminus of a camel route that brought Arabia to Black Africa, developing from a modest 11th-century Tuareg trading post into a major financial centre and one of the most famous sites of Islamic scholarship in the Muslim world. Its wealth, like that of many Sahelian towns straddling the trans-Sahara trade routes, was based largely on gold, salt, ivory, kola nuts and slaves. Its decline from a city of 100,000 souls began when it was captured and sacked in 1591 by the Berber armies of Sultan Mansour of Marrakesh and when Europe's maritime nations began foraying along the coast of West Africa, breaking the Tuareg's monopoly on trans-Sahara trade.

Wandering through the narrow twisting streets of the old section of Timbuktu, travellers will see two and three-storey mud houses with huge wooden doors ornamented with studs and carvings, bread being baked in dome-shaped ovens, three famous mosques, the houses where three feisty

http://www.lonelyplanet.com

LONELY PLANET GUIDES TO AFRICA

Africa on a shoestring
From Marrakesh to Kampala, Mozambique to Mauritania, Johannesburg to Cairo – this guidebook has all the facts on travelling in Africa. Comprehensive information on more than 50 countries.

Arabic (Egyptian) phrasebook
This handy phrasebook is packed with words and phrases to cover almost every situation. Arabic script is included making this phrasebook useful to travellers in most other Arabic-speaking countries.

Arabic (Moroccan) phrasebook
Whether finding a hotel or asking for a meal, this indispensable phrasebook will help travellers to North Africa make their travels with ease. This phrasebook also includes Arabic script and a helpful pronunciation guide.

Cape Town city guide
Cape Town offers lively cafés, magnificent surf beaches and superb mountain walks. This indispensable guide is packed with insider tips for both business and leisure travellers.

Central Africa
This guide tells where to go to meet gorillas in the jungle, how to catch a steamer down the Congo...even the best beer to wash down grilled boa constrictor! Covers Cameroun, the Central African Republic, Chad, the Congo, Equatorial Guinea, Gabon, São Tomé & Principe, and Zaïre.

East Africa
Detailed information on Kenya, Uganda, Rwanda, Burundi, eastern Zaïre and Tanzania. The latest edition includes a 32-page full-colour Safari Guide.

Egypt
This guide takes you into and beyond the spectacular and mysterious pyramids, temples, tombs, monasteries, mosques and bustling main streets of Egypt.

Ethiopian (Amharic) phrasebook
You'll enjoy Ethiopia a whole lot more if you can speak some of the language. All the phrases you need are at your fingertips in this handy phrasebook.

Kenya
This superb guide features a 32-page Safari Guide with colour photographs, illustrations and information on East Africa's famous wildlife.

Morocco
This thoroughly revised and expanded guide is full of down-to-earth information and reliable advice for every budget. It includes a 20-page colour section on Moroccan arts and crafts and information on trekking routes in the High Atlas and Rif Mountains.

North Africa
A most detailed and comprehensive guide to the Maghreb – Morocco, Algeria, Tunisia and Libya. It points the way to fascinating bazaars, superb beaches and the vast Sahara, and is packed with reliable advice for every budget. This new guide includes a 20-page full colour section on Moroccan arts and crafts.

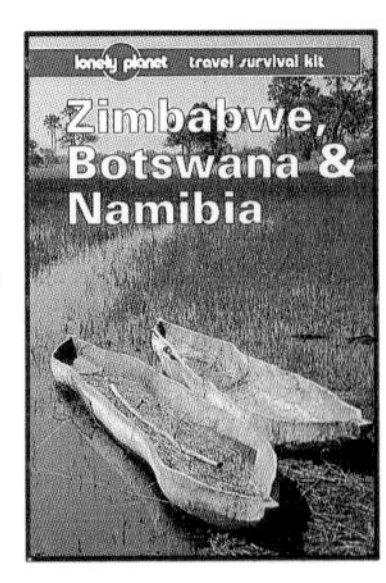

South Africa, Lesotho & Swaziland
Travel to southern Africa and you'll be surprised by its cultural diversity and incredible beauty. There's no better place to see Africa's amazing wildlife. All the essential travel details are included in this guide as well as information about wildlife reserves, and a 32-page full colour Safari Guide.

Swahili phrasebook
Swahili is a major lingua franca of the African continent. This handy phrasebook will prove invaluable for travellers to Africa.

Trekking in East Africa
Practical, first-hand information for trekkers for a region renowned for its spectacular national parks and rewarding trekking trails. Covers treks in Kenya, Tanzania, Uganda and Malawi.

West Africa
All the necessary information for independent travel in Benin, Burkino Faso, Cape Verde, Côte d'Ivoire, The Gambia, Ghana, Guinea, Guinea-Bissau, Liberia, Mali, Mauritania, Niger, Nigeria, Senegal, Sierra Leone and Togo. Includes a colour section on local culture and birdlife.

Zimbabwe, Botswana & Namibia
Exotic wildlife, breathtaking scenery and fascinating people...this comprehensive guide shows a wilder, older side of Africa for the adventurous traveller. Includes a 32-page colour Safari Guide.

LONELY PLANET PRODUCTS

AFRICA

Africa on a shoestring • Arabic (Moroccan) phrasebook • Cape Town city guide • Central Africa • East Africa • Egypt • Egypt travel atlas • Ethiopian (Amharic) phrasebook • Kenya • Kenya travel atlas • Morocco • North Africa • South Africa, Lesotho & Swaziland • South Africa, Lesotho & Swaziland travel atlas •Swahili phrasebook • Trekking in East Africa• West Africa • Zimbabwe, Botswana & Namibia • Zimbabwe, Botswana & Namibia travel atlas

Travel Literature: The Rainbird: A Central African Journey • Songs to an African Sunset: A Zimbabwean Story

ANTARCTICA

Antarctica

AUSTRALIA & THE PACIFIC

Australia • Australian phrasebook • Bushwalking in Australia • Bushwalking in Papua New Guinea • Fiji • Fijian phrasebook • Islands of Australia's Great Barrier Reef • Melbourne city guide • Micronesia • New Caledonia • New South Wales & the ACT • New Zealand • Northern Territory • Outback Australia • Papua New Guinea • Papua New Guinea phrasebook • Queensland • Rarotonga & the Cook Islands • Samoa • Solomon Islands • South Australia • Sydney city guide • Tahiti & French Polynesia • Tasmania • Tonga • Tramping in New Zealand • Vanuatu • Victoria • Western Australia

Travel Literature: Islands in the Clouds • Sean & David's Long Drive

CENTRAL AMERICA & THE CARIBBEAN

Bermuda • Central America on a shoestring • Costa Rica • Cuba • Eastern Caribbean • Guatemala, Belize & Yucatán: La Ruta Maya • Jamaica

EUROPE

Austria • Baltic States & Kaliningrad • Baltics States phrasebook • Britain • Central Europe on a shoestring • Central Europe phrasebook • Czech & Slovak Republics • Denmark • Dublin city guide • Eastern Europe on a shoestring • Eastern Europe phrasebook • Finland • France • Greece • Greek phrasebook • Hungary • Iceland, Greenland & the Faroe Islands • Ireland • Italy • Mediterranean Europe on a shoestring • Mediterranean Europe phrasebook • Paris city guide • Poland • Prague city guide • Russia, Ukraine & Belarus • Russian phrasebook • Scandinavian & Baltic Europe on a shoestring • Scandinavian Europe phrasebook • Slovenia • St Petersburg city guide • Switzerland • Trekking in Greece • Trekking in Spain • Ukrainian phrasebook • Vienna city guide • Walking in Britain • Walking in Switzerland • Western Europe on a shoestring • Western Europe phrasebook

INDIAN SUBCONTINENT

Bangladesh • Bengali phrasebook • Delhi city guide • Hindi/Urdu phrasebook • India • India & Bangladesh travel atlas • Indian Himalaya • Karakoram Highway • Nepal • Nepali phrasebook • Pakistan • Sri Lanka • Sri Lanka phrasebook • Trekking in the Indian Himalaya • Trekking in the Karakoram & Hindukush • Trekking in the Nepal Himalaya

Travel Literature: In Rajasthan • Shopping for Buddhas

ISLANDS OF THE INDIAN OCEAN

Madagascar & Comoros • Maldives & Islands of the East Indian Ocean • Mauritius, Réunion & Seychelles

MIDDLE EAST & CENTRAL ASIA

Arab Gulf States • Arabic (Egyptian) phrasebook • Central Asia • Iran • Israel & the Palestinian Territories • Israel & the Palestinian Territories travel atlas • Jordan & Syria • Jordan, Syria & Lebanon travel atlas • Middle East • Turkey • Turkish phrasebook • Yemen

Travel Literature: The Gates of Damascus • Kingdom of the Film Stars: Journey into Jordan

NORTH AMERICA

Alaska • Backpacking in Alaska • Baja California • California & Nevada • Canada • Florida • Hawaii • Honolulu city guide • Los Angeles city guide • Mexico • Miami city guide • New England • New Orleans city guide • Pacific Northwest USA • Rocky Mountain States • San Francisco city guide • Southwest USA • USA phrasebook

NORTH-EAST ASIA

Beijing city guide • Cantonese phrasebook • China • Hong Kong city guide • Hong Kong, Macau & Guangzhou • Japan • Japanese phrasebook • Japanese audio pack • Korea • Korean phrasebook • Mandarin phrasebook • Mongolia • Mongolian phrasebook • North-East Asia on a shoestring • Seoul city guide • Taiwan • Tibet • Tibet phrasebook • Tokyo city guide

Travel Literature: Lost Japan

SOUTH AMERICA

Argentina, Uruguay & Paraguay • Bolivia • Brazil • Brazilian phrasebook • Buenos Aires city guide • Chile & Easter Island • Chile & Easter Island travel atlas • Colombia • Ecuador & the Galápagos Islands • Latin American Spanish phrasebook • Peru • Quechua phrasebook • Rio de Janeiro city guide • South America on a shoestring • Trekking in the Patagonian Andes • Venezuela

Travel Literature: Full Circle: A South American Journey

SOUTH-EAST ASIA

Bali & Lombok • Bangkok city guide • Burmese phrasebook• Cambodia • Ho Chi Minh city guide • Indonesia • Indonesian phrasebook • Indonesian audio pack • Jakarta city guide • Java • Laos • Laos travel atlas • Lao phrasebook • Malaysia, Singapore & Brunei • Myanmar (Burma) • Philippines • Pilipino phrasebook • Singapore city guide • South-East Asia on a shoestring • South-East Asia phrasebook • Thailand • Thailand travel atlas • Thai phrasebook • Thai Hill Tribes phrasebook • Thai audio pack • Vietnam • Vietnamese phrasebook • Vietnam travel atlas

LONELY PLANET TRAVEL ATLASES

Conventional fold-out maps work just fine when you're planning your trip on the kitchen table, but have you ever tried to use one – or the half-dozen you sometimes need to cover a country – while you're actually on the road? Even if you have the origami skills necessary to unfold the sucker, you know that flimsy bit of paper is not going to last the distance.

"Lonely Planet travel atlases are designed to make it through your journey in one piece – the sturdy book format is based on the assumption that since all travellers want to make it home without punctures, tears or wrinkles, the maps they use should too."

The travel atlases contain detailed, colour maps that are checked on the road by our travel authors to ensure their accuracy. Place name spellings are consistent with our associated guidebooks, so you can use the atlas and the guidebook hand in hand as you travel and find what you are looking for. Unlike conventional maps, each atlas has a comprehensive index, as well as a detailed legend and helpful 'getting around' sections translated into five languages. Sorry, no free steak knives...

Features of this series include:

- full-colour maps, plus colour photos
- maps researched and checked by Lonely Planet authors
- place names correspond with Lonely Planet guidebooks, so there are no confusing spelling differences
- complete index of features and place names
- atlas legend and travelling information presented in five languages: English, French, German, Spanish and Japanese

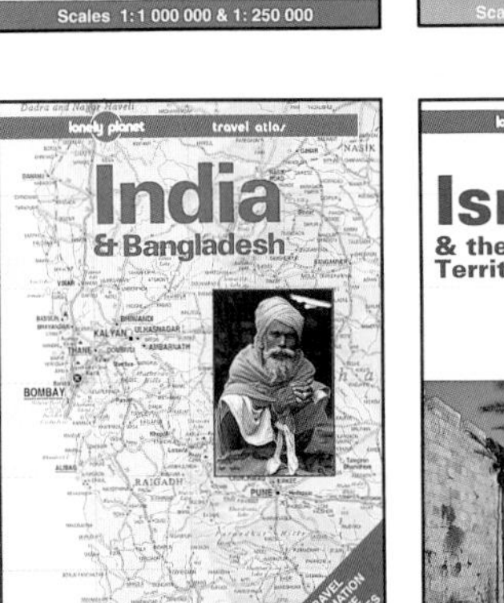

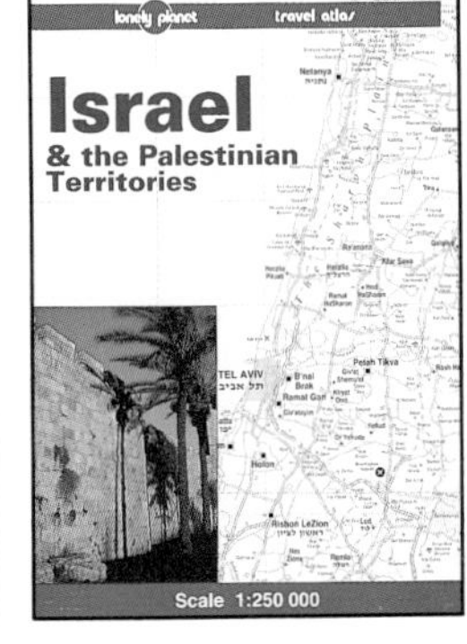

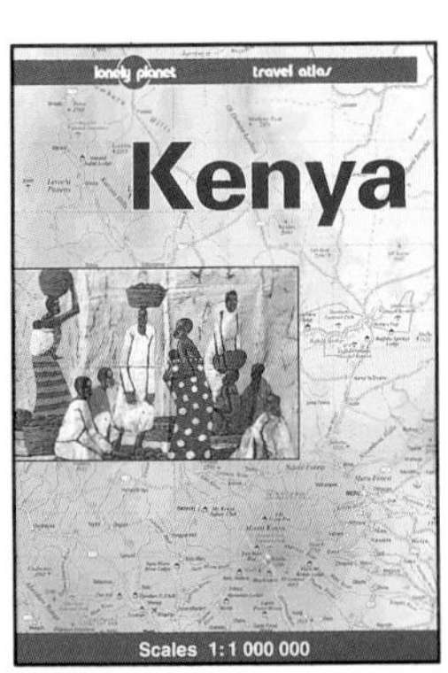

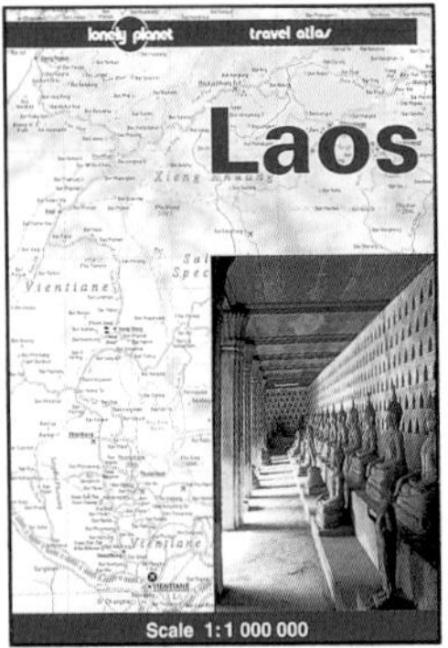

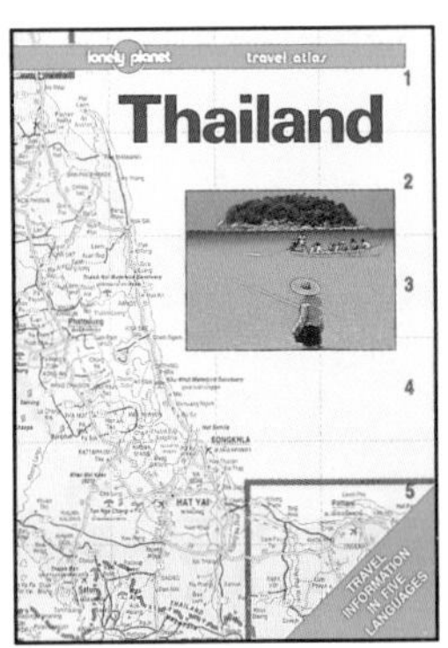

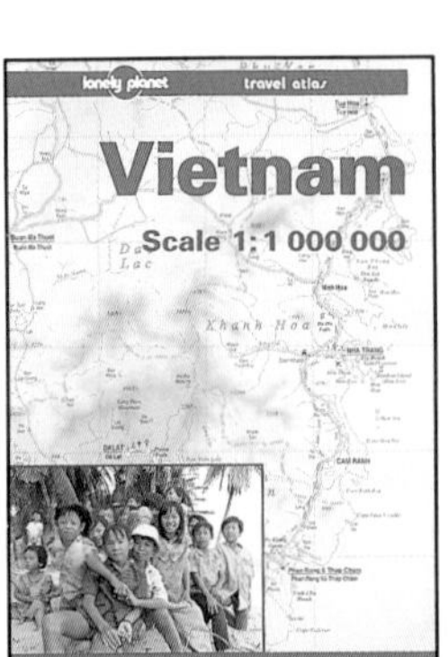

THE LONELY PLANET STORY

Lonely Planet published its first book in 1973 in response to the numerous 'How did you do it?' questions Maureen and Tony Wheeler were asked after driving, bussing, hitching, sailing and railing their way from England to Australia.

Written at a kitchen table and hand collated, trimmed and stapled, *Across Asia on the Cheap* became an instant local bestseller, inspiring thoughts of another book.

Eighteen months in South-East Asia resulted in their second guide, *South-East Asia on a shoestring*, which they put together in a backstreet Chinese hotel in Singapore in 1975. The 'yellow bible', as it quickly became known to backpackers around the world, soon became *the* guide to the region. It has sold well over half a million copies and is now in its 8th edition, still retaining its familiar yellow cover.

Today there are over 180 titles, including travel guides, walking guides, language kits & phrasebooks, travel atlases and travel literature. The company is one of the largest travel publishers in the world. Although Lonely Planet initially specialised in guides to Asia, we now cover most regions of the world, including the Pacific, North America, South America, Africa, the Middle East and Europe.

The emphasis continues to be on travel for independent travellers. Tony and Maureen still travel for several months of each year and play an active part in the writing, updating and quality control of Lonely Planet's guides.

They have been joined by over 70 authors and 170 staff at our offices in Melbourne (Australia), Oakland (USA), London (UK) and Paris (France). Travellers themselves also make a valuable contribution to the guides through the feedback we receive in thousands of letters each year.

The people at Lonely Planet strongly believe that travellers can make a positive contribution to the countries they visit, both through their appreciation of the countries' culture, wildlife and natural features, and through the money they spend. In addition, the company makes a direct contribution to the countries and regions it covers. Since 1986 a percentage of the income from each book has been donated to ventures such as famine relief in Africa; aid projects in India; agricultural projects in Central America; Greenpeace's efforts to halt French nuclear testing in the Pacific; and Amnesty International.

'I hope we send people out with the right attitude about travel. You realise when you travel that there are so many different perspectives about the world, so we hope these books will make people more interested in what they see.'

– Tony Wheeler

LONELY PLANET PUBLICATIONS

AUSTRALIA (HEAD OFFICE)
PO Box 617, Hawthorn 3122, Victoria
tel: (03) 9819 1877 fax: (03) 9819 6459
e-mail: talk2us@lonelyplanet.com.au

UK
10 Barley Mow Passage,
Chiswick, London W4 4PH
tel: (0181) 742 3161 fax: (0181) 742 2772
e-mail: 100413.3551@compuserve.com

USA
Embarcadero West,155 Filbert St, Suite 251,
Oakland, CA 94607
tel: (510) 893 8555 TOLL FREE: 800 275-8555
fax: (510) 893 8563
e-mail: info@lonelyplanet.com

FRANCE
71 bis rue du Cardinal Lemoine, 75005 Paris
tel: 1 44 32 06 20 fax: 1 46 34 72 55
e-mail: 100560.415@compuserve.com

World Wide Web: http://www.lonelyplanet.com/

SOUTH AFRICA, LESOTHO & SWAZILAND TRAVEL ATLAS

Dear Traveller,

We would appreciate it if you would take the time to write your thoughts on this page and return it to a Lonely Planet office. Only with your help can we continue to make sure this atlas is as accurate and travel-friendly as possible.

Where did you acquire this atlas?

Bookstore ☐ In which section of the store did you find it, i.e. maps or travel guidebooks? ....

Map shop ☐ Direct mail ☐ Other ....

How are you using this travel atlas?

On the road ☐ For home reference ☐ For business reference ☐

Other ....

When travelling with this atlas, did you find any inaccuracies?

....

....

....

How does the atlas fare on the road in terms of ease of use and durability?

....

Are you using the atlas in conjunction with an LP guidebook/s? Yes ☐ No ☐

Which one/s?..

Have you bought any other LP products for your trip?..

Do you think the information on the travel atlas maps is presented clearly? Yes ☐ No ☐

If English is not your main language, do you find the language sections useful? Yes ☐ No ☐

Please list any features you think should be added to the travel atlas.

....

....

....

Would you consider purchasing another atlas in this series? Yes ☐ No ☐

Please indicate your age group.

15-25 ☐ 26-35 ☐ 36-45 ☐ 46-55 ☐ 56-65 ☐ 66+ ☐

Do you have any other general comments you'd like to make?

....

....

....

....

....

P.S. Thank you very much for this information. The best contributions will be rewarded with a free copy of a Lonely Planet book. We give away lots of books, but, unfortunately, not every contributor receives one.

Notes